Finally... I'm A Doctor

Finally...
I'm A Doctor

Neil Shulman M.D.

CHARLES SCRIBNER'S SONS
NEW YORK

Published in cooperation with
Hemisphere Publishing Corporation

1 3 5 7 9 11 13 15 17 19 H/C 20 18 16 14 12 10 8 6 4 2

Printed in the United States of America
Library of Congress Catalog Card Number 76-14605
ISBN 0-684-14601-0

To Mom, Dad, Grandmother, and Essie

I am indebted to my good friends
Carl Hiaasen, Barbara Davis, and Bill Begell
for their help with this book.

FOREWORD

The events portrayed in this book are a collection of incidents in my past and in the pasts of other doctors across the United States. They are fictional only in the sense that the characters are not actual persons, but merely types of personalities. However, all the episodes have their basis in reality.

The practice of medicine is, of course, a serious business. However, medical training, seen through the eyes of the naive, idealistic young people who comprise the majority of students who enter the profession, is a bewildering, often absurd experience. A unique sense of humor is demanded of all who want to survive. In this book I have tried to recapture that unsophisticated perspective and that distinctive brand of humor.

I hope, however, that I have gone beyond what is humorous in medical training. There is another side to the system of medical education in the U.S. today. Those same idealistic young people who enter premed programs seldom graduate from medical school with their idealism intact. The frustrations they encounter—the fierce competition, the oppressive tuition rates, and the all-too-frequent failure of medical science to forestall death—mold their attitudes in a way they had never intended.

I hope the readers of this book will acquire an

increased understanding of the diverse factors involved in the "education" of a doctor. The forces which affect the development of physicians directly influence the health care system in the country today.

Finally... I'm A Doctor

1

I had spent four years of high school preparing for premed. I wanted to be a doctor more than anything else in the world. I had spent those same four years of high school preparing to ask Cheryl Seltzer for a date. I wanted her body only slightly less than I wanted to be a doctor.

Cheryl Seltzer's body was the talk of the entire student population, both male and female. As a mere schoolmate, I didn't have a prayer; but as a premed, things were different. Not that Cheryl Seltzer suddenly found me irresistible; her mother did.

I disliked Mrs. Seltzer intensely. In fact, she drove me insane. What really got to me was that Mrs. Seltzer found me simply enchanting. Every week, for as long as I could remember, Mrs. Seltzer had come to my house to play bridge with "the girls." Every week she had begged me to become a doctor, and every week she had recommended I date her daughter. Now, although I knew I was becoming a doctor *in spite of* Mrs. Seltzer, she was convinced she had inspired my decision. And, although God knows my attraction to Cheryl Seltzer was in no way connected to her mother, Mrs. Seltzer took every opportunity to remind me she had simply "planted a seed" and was now watching it grow.

I had been a premed less than a week when Mrs.

Seltzer invited me out to dinner. It was during one of the weekly bridge games that she dangled the bait.

"It's in celebration of Mr. Seltzer's birthday," she explained. "Of course, Cheryl will be there."

I accepted on the spot.

I should have known better. Not only was I forced to endure an entire evening of Mrs. Seltzer's incessant chatter, but her daughter (whose presence made me extremely nervous) barely deigned to acknowledge my existence. As I said before, Cheryl wasn't exactly falling all over herself trying to get me to ask her for a date, but my premed status did pull enough weight to persuade her to tolerate her mother's scheme. In fact, she found the whole thing highly amusing and didn't bother to conceal her mirth.

The prevailing topic of conversation was Mrs. Seltzer's favorite—my becoming a doctor.

"I've always wished that I had married a doctor," she said with a significant glance at Cheryl. Mr. Seltzer was in insurance. "Heaven knows I tried. In college, I would always study in the med library. But the way those med students study is positively insulting. I mean, they concentrate!" Then, recalling my new position, she turned to me all smiles, "I'm sure you won't be like that, Lloyd."

I squirmed uncomfortably in my seat. Mrs. Seltzer's two-edged compliments always left me feeling uneasy.

"Lloyd," she interrupted herself, "don't eat so many rolls. You won't have room for dinner."

I glanced at the bread basket and discovered, to my extreme embarrassment, that only one roll remained.

2

Since I had been the only one to indulge, I concluded that I must have been eating in pace with Mrs. Seltzer's chattering. In my nervousness, I had been unaware of my bad manners, but kindly Mrs. Seltzer had been nice enough to alert me—and everyone else. I could have sworn that Cheryl's gorgeous eyes were laughing at me, but when I glanced in her direction, she seemed to be looking right through me instead.

Mrs. Seltzer continued her saga: "Then I tried faking illness—just a harmless feminine strategy," she smiled coyly. "I held the record of sophomore girls for time spent in the infirmary. Lloyd, please don't sip your soup so loudly. You know, as a future doctor you should acquire some social poise."

I blushed, avoiding Cheryl's eyes.

"Well, anyway," Mrs. Seltzer continued, "I finally turned to candy-striping. That's how I met Leo." Now she smiled at Mr. Seltzer who all through the preceding conversation had been glancing furtively from side to side as if looking for an escape. "A drunken driver knocked Leo down. We met while he was in the hospital recuperating. I couldn't help falling for Leo. He's so sweet—even if he isn't a doctor."

Well that's big of her, I thought.

"And now," she concluded, misty eyed, "my only wish is that my daughter will enjoy the happiness I've missed."

At this point, I choked. My intentions toward Cheryl were in no way honorable and this last remark was an obvious threat to my freedom.

"You know, Lloyd," Mrs. Seltzer turned to me with an air of conspiracy, "you're a very smart young man. You know where your future lies. Why, when you're a doctor, you'll be set for life. Please, dear, don't eat so fast. It's bad for the digestion."

I had already developed a bad case of indigestion, not from eating too fast, but from listening to Mrs. Seltzer. Assuming my values coincided with hers was Mrs. Seltzer's most annoying habit. She wanted me to be a doctor so I could be rich and successful and marry her daughter. I wasn't exactly sure why I wanted to be a doctor, but I was resisting those very temptations. When Mrs. Seltzer spoke to me as if we were on the same wavelength, it was all I could bear. I felt my temper rise and I struggled with my self-control to avoid saying anything I would regret later. Just then the waiter arrived with the check, rescuing me from a bad attack of nerves. I offered to halve the fare with Mr. Seltzer, but Mrs. Seltzer wouldn't hear of it. To Cheryl's amusement and my humiliation, she leaned close to Mr. Seltzer and whispered in a voice loud enough to be heard two tables away: "Just consider it an investment in our daughter's future, dear."

And so the evening went. I had suffered through dinner, praying that Mrs. Seltzer would at least have the decency to leave Cheryl and me alone when it was over. But no. She insisted we join them for coffee back at the Seltzer home. I sat through another two hours of Mrs. Seltzer's nonsense. It was all I could take. I had to say goodnight to Cheryl under the watchful eye of her mother.

Mrs. Seltzer was definitely going to be a problem—to say nothing of her daughter. However, I was determined to have my way with Cheryl if it was the last thing I ever did.

4

2

Getting into premed hadn't been easy. To this day, I think of it as an initiation—a forewarning of worse things to come.

First of all there was that 480 on my SAT Verbals. A 480 could have kept me out of premed. My initial reaction to my distressing score was righteous indignation:

"The gross injustice of it all!" I cried. I was presenting my case to the family at breakfast after a sleepless night during which I had contemplated everything from dentistry to suicide. In the morning I knew I still wanted to be a doctor. "Why should verbal scores count so much? I want to practice medicine, not write a book."

"That may be true, Lloyd," said my father. "But students should be well-rounded, with ability in both language skills *and* science. Med schools don't want to produce narrow-minded doctors who only think medicine."

I was stunned. I couldn't believe my father was capable of treason.

"Lloyd, please be home early for dinner tonight. We're having a guest," my mother said.

How could she think of dinner at a time like this? My parents were turning against me in my hour of need. I resolved to be late for dinner.

5

When I finally returned home that night, dessert was being served. I plied this information from my little brother Edward who was leaving for baseball practice just as I came in. I sauntered into the dining room, ready to embarrass my parents in front of whoever it was they considered so much more important than me.

"Hello, Mother. Father," I said in the most careless tone I could muster. "So sorry I'm late." At this point, the guest, who had been sitting with his back towards me, turned around. "David Kaplan!" I gasped.

David Kaplan was a premed student two years older than myself. He was charming, he was brilliant, and he was the darling of every Jewish mother and father in my parents' social set. In short, he was a pain in the ass. I had been administered daily doses of David Kaplan since the age of thirteen. He did everything better than I, and my parents never let me forget it. Captain of the debating team, president of the senior class, National Merit finalist—all this and more was David Kaplan. David had scored 800 on *his* SAT's and now he was breezing his way through premed. Was it fair play on my parents' part to invite my boyhood rival to dinner at a time when my self-esteem was at an all time low? No, it was not.

"Hello, Lloyd," David said, smiling in his obnoxiously charming way as he glanced at the kitchen clock. In addition to his other merits, David was never late for dinner.

"Hi," I mumbled, slumping into my chair.

"Lloyd, David's doing just wonderfully in school," my mother said as she served the banana cake.

6

I glared at my mother as David said, "Lloyd, your parents tell me you're considering premed."

"That's right," I said, somewhat defensively.

"David thinks you can get in—even with a 480," my father said.

"*Even* with a 480?" I echoed in mock horror.

"Sure," said David, "not very many people are outstanding in both science *and* liberal arts."

Except, of course, David Kaplan, I raged inwardly.

"Lloyd, David will be glad to help you once you're in. Your father and I have discussed the matter with him. We're willing to pay him for his trouble."

I froze, my fork suspended midway between my mouth and my plate. So that was the underlying purpose of this dinner. David Kaplan tutor me? Over my dead body. My scores were low, but even so, I could make it through premed without any help.

"I'll make it through on my own," I asserted.

David, Mom, and Dad were obviously startled by my tone of voice.

"Of course you will," said David after an uncomfortable moment of silence. "And when you come right down to it, determination is half the battle. I admire your spirit, Lloyd."

David was an old pro at extricating himself from embarrassing situations. Naturally, my father ate up every word David said and, beaming with pride, added, "Lloyd, I think you should stop by my old fraternity house this weekend."

"Absolutely," David agreed. "Premeds need fraternity life more for educational purposes than for the

7

social aspects of it. In every fraternity the old exams are filed and released only to dues-paying members."

Apparently, these three were convinced that I faced certain failure if I didn't find help somewhere. I agreed to the visit much to the relief of my worried parents.

By the time dessert was over, my career was decided, my grades were determined, and my social life was directed toward fraternity row. For some reason, I didn't sleep any better that night than the night before.

Saturday morning found me at my father's fraternity house, on the campus of City University. After a few preliminary questions, I was directed to the rush chairman. The rush chairman is really the fraternity's PR man; he's responsible for recruiting raw freshmen. I wasn't a freshman yet, but he gave me the red-carpet treatment anyway.

"Hello, Goldman," he said. "So your father's an EAP alumnus and you're thinking of joining?"

"Well, I haven't been officially accepted yet," I admitted. "I'm applying for premed."

"Then you've come to the right frat. EAP has got the most complete exam file on campus. Our exams go back as far as '47."

I tried to look suitably impressed. He showed me around the house and introduced me to a few of the guys, all of whom assured me EAP could supply plenty of hot chicks and old exams.

When I left EAP, I visited its biggest rival—ASE.

"Hello, Goldman," said ASE's rush chairman. "So you're thinking of joining a fraternity?"

"I haven't been accepted yet," I replied. "I'm applying for premed."

"Then you've come to the right frat. ASE has got the most complete exam file on campus. Our exams go back as far as '47 . . . ."

Before leaving that day, I visited four other fraternities. In each, a carbon copy of every other rush chairman assured me that his fraternity had the oldest exam files on campus. I could see premed was going to be a rat race.

And it was. Exam files weren't very helpful. The only guarantee for passing a course was to really know the material. Knowing the material meant getting to class a half hour early in order to get a front row seat. It meant copying in detail every list, diagram, and formula written on the board prior to class. It meant knowing by heart the professor's home phone number and address, as well as that of his next of kin, in case he was to expire while grading finals. It meant furiously scribbling notes while worrying whether strength or paper supply would give out first. It meant another fifteen minutes talking to the professor after class about things that had nothing to do with his course. And it meant convincing premed competitors to lend their notes for fill-ins.

For many students, cut-throat competition—from admission to graduation—is what premed is all about. A lot of students never get in; some drop out along the way. Those who make it have only passed the first hurdle on the formidable path leading to practice as an M.D.

3

My Grandmother Schlessel had decided that her grandson Lloyd Goldman was an M.D. long before I entered college. According to family legend, I was only five months old on that fateful spring day when Grandmother took me for a carriage stroll through the park. There she happened to run into an old friend, Mrs. Sternbach, who was also out for a stroll with her baby grandson.

"Mrs. Schlessel," said Mrs. Sternbach, "meet my grandson Mark—the lawyer."

"Delighted," replied my grandmother. "And I'd like for you to meet my grandson Lloyd—the doctor."

Grandmother Schlessel was my mother's mother and had the typical appearance of every elderly matron who spends half the day knitting sweaters for her grandchildren and the other half baking cookies in anticipation of their next visit. But Grandmother was much more than that, for behind those wire-rimmed glasses and beneath that kindly expression ticked a brain endowed with one of the most amazing combinations of business acumen, computer matchmaking, and prying curiosity I've ever encountered.

Grandmother subscribed to all three local newspapers. But not because she had nothing to do but read. She first scanned the obituary columns and then turned

11

to the classified "real estate for sale" sections. Her target was the "little old widow homeowners" who were easiest to deal with. Somehow, she always had the inside scoop on which residential blocks were in demand by big apartment syndicate firms. My grandmother realized that the little old widow types were often hesitant to deal with shifty real estate operators. So sweet innocent grandmother would visit the widows early, buy their property at a somewhat reduced rate, and then resell to the shrewd syndicators at a considerable profit. Grandmother did have a conscience though, and making the loot wasn't half as important as keeping her reputation clean. She would, without hesitation, split her profit with the original owner.

In addition, her matchmaking talent was known nationwide and thirty-two couples throughout the country had been bound in wedlock thanks to her efforts. She claimed a 5 percent divorce rate, considerably below the national average.

Typical of my grandmother's zeal for the medical profession was the time she decided to take me to the famous Bamberg's Delicatessen to celebrate my admission to premed. It was about noon on a Friday. The raunchy lunch-hour crew was mobbing Mr. Bamberg's entrance. Standing between the bakery counter and the meat counter were twenty-five starving souls waiting for seats. The meat cutter, a sadist at heart, enjoyed watching the people who stood between the strawberry cobblers and the slices of corn beef drool while they waited.

My grandmother never let herself be manipulated. Protected by her wire-rimmed glasses, she made her way past cigar-smoking executives and long-legged secretaries straight to the front of the line. She chose a booth for four that was already occupied by three and asked, in a grandmotherly way, if the three gentlemen wouldn't mind being joined. They consented politely. Who could refuse a nice old lady? Defying the laws of logic, Grandmother (no Slenderella herself) squeezed in beside the two heavyset gentlemen, leaving myself and the third man, a stringbean, in the opposite seat.

To add verbal imposition to physical discomfort, Grandmother proudly announced, "Gentlemen, I would like for you to meet my grandson, Dr. Lloyd Goldman."

Grandmother was always introducing me as her Grandson the Doctor and it usually put me in a very embarrassing position. This time was no exception. I looked younger than my eighteen years and my long hair and jeans didn't exactly project the image of a professional. The three men glanced at each other and, barely repressing their laughter, replied in unison: "Now, that's very interesting. We're physicians ourselves."

Grandmother bit her tongue and I smiled wanly. Well that figures, I thought to myself. It was bound to happen sooner or later.

Enjoying our discomfort, the doctor to my left continued, "I'm Dr. Harris. And my colleagues are Dr. Stone and Dr. Tauben. We're attending a medical convention here in Washington."

Now Grandmother did what she always did when she found herself in a compromising situation of her own making—she passed the buck. Suddenly, she was completely engrossed by her surroundings. An innocent

13

passerby would have thought that here was an old lady who had never seen the inside of a restaurant before. There was now an impenetrable sound barrier surrounding my grandmother. Of course, this left me holding the ball.

I can fix Grandmother once and for all, I told myself, if I just tell these men the doctor routine is all her idea. But she'd never forgive me and it will probably be a cold day in August before I taste her potato pancakes again. That last consideration weighted the scales in Grandmother's favor. I politely inquired about the medical convention.

"In fact, we were just discussing it," replied Dr. Harris.

Naturally.

"This morning our group held a debate on recent advances in coronary artery bypass procedures. Are you familiar with the literature?"

Was he kidding? I couldn't even spell it. It was time to teach Grandmother a lesson. And, besides, I could live without potato pancakes. I decided to take a moral stand on the issue. One look at Grandmother's sweetly smiling face, however, changed my mind. I just couldn't do that to my own grandmother. Again I gave in, but I refused to resort to lying. Instead, I simply grunted in a way that could be interpreted as either a yes or a no. There were some points on which I refused to compromise—potato pancakes or no.

"I presented a paper proving that coronary artery bypass with the femoral vein has proven to be successful in relieving the pain of angina pectoris," said Dr. Tauben.

"There's really no disagreement about that," said Dr. Stone.

"Of course not," I piped in, seizing the opportunity to say something without really saying anything. Grandmother's sparkling smile was beginning to irritate me.

Dr. Stone continued, "The question is whether bypass procedure is successful in preventing an acute myocardial infarction and prolonging life."

"That certainly *is* the issue," I said. I saw Dr. Stone snicker into his water glass. Would he reprimand me for impersonating a doctor? I steeled myself for the ordeal, but to my surprise he winked at me and continued the discussion.

We played the game for a few minutes longer until a glance at Grandmother's face told me she had had enough. Being a successful businesswoman, she was sensitive to the moods and motives of other people. She knew when she was being humored, however kindly, and she didn't like it one bit.

"Well, Dr. Goldman," said Dr. Stone, "I'm impressed by your thorough comprehension of a very complicated medical problem . . ."

"Excuse us, gentlemen," Grandmother interrupted coldly, "but I've just spotted an old friend and I'd like to say hello."

I had just enough time to breathe a sigh of relief before Grandmother and I were halfway across the room, approaching her friend's table.

"Mrs. Sternbach, hello," called Grandmother. "You'll never guess," she continued without stopping to take a breath. "Just this moment a delegation of doctors was consulting my Lloyd . . ."

Grandmother would never learn.

4

Sneaking a dissected fetal pig out of biology lab was not nearly as risky as getting the specimen into the basement of a kosher home.

My freshman year was nearly over and my last quiz was a lab examination on the anatomy of a full term fetal pig. I had easy B's in all my other courses, but in biology, I was on the B-C borderline. This was a dangerous predicament for a premed student.

My premed neighbor, Herman Tuttman, was determined to ace the biology exam. He had a plan and I was to help. He brought a plastic bag, a roll of toilet paper, and a five-ounce bottle of after-shave to class. Herman wrapped the dissected fetal pig in the toilet paper and sprinkled the remains with the shaving lotion. Carrying the embalmed pig in the plastic bag, we left for Herman's house.

When we reached the bus stop, Herman turned to me and said, "OK, Lloyd, now *you* carry the bag."

"Not me," I protested. The after-shave hadn't been very effective and the pig reeked of formaldehyde.

"Lloyd, do you want to pass this exam or not? Since I've done all the work, I think the least you can do is carry the bag."

We hopped on the first bus that came along. Carrying the bag, I made my way to the back of the bus, accompanied by ugly looks and snide remarks.

"Something smells queer."

"There should be a law against letting people like that on a city bus."

"Young man, when was the last time you had a bath?"

I took the very last seat on the bus and sat next to the window which I opened wide. Meanwhile, Herman took a seat in the front of the bus and joined the other passengers in complaining about "that awful smell."

Why am I doing this, I wondered. I knew the answer. I needed that B and I was willing to endure almost anything to get it. If I got a C, my dream of becoming a doctor would be ended.

I don't care what anyone says, I told myself. My future is in this bag. I have a moral obligation to learn each and every structure of this pig. Some day, a life will be hanging by a thread and my knowledge of the anatomy of a fetal pig, the anatomy of a *full-term* fetal pig, will save that life. What these ungrateful people are witnessing is the genesis of a distinguished medical career . . .

"Do yourself a favor kid and get off 'dis bus."

"Wh . . . what?"

"You heard me."

The gum-chewing, leather-jacketed young man who had so rudely interrupted my thoughts extended his rather muscular arm and helped me to my feet. I found myself face to face with his chest. I decided it was a nice day for a walk and left the bus through the nearest exit. I began walking. When I reached the next bus stop, there was Herman.

"What are you trying to pull, Goldman?" he cried. "That's *my* pig. *I'm* going to ace the test."

"Calm down, Herman," I said. "No one's trying to steal your pig. Since you're so concerned, you carry it now."

We walked the rest of the way to Herman's house where our next obstacle was getting the pig into Herman's basement-turned-laboratory.

"What's in the bag?" asked his mother.

"Porno," Herman replied.

His mother laughed and turned to me. "That Herman, what a sense of humor! Now, Lloyd, how about some dinner? I've made roast beef."

I was familiar with Mrs. Tuttman's dinners and I knew that tonight, of all nights, I couldn't afford to be fattened like a calf for slaughter. However, I accepted her kind invitation merely to divert her attention from Herman who slipped unnoticed down the basement stairs. He returned without his package and we sat down to dinner with Mr. and Mrs. Tuttman. Really, we sat down to dinner with Mr. Tuttman. Mrs. Tuttman spent her dinner hour trotting from kitchen to dining room and back again.

Appetizers consisted of gefilte fish on a wedge of lettuce followed by matza ball soup. I love gefilte fish and I love matza ball soup. Throwing caution to the wind, I devoured both.

I had no sooner raised my head from my empty soup bowl when the doors to the Tuttman kitchen swung open and Mrs. Tuttman entered bearing a platter of roast beef. She set the plate on the table and proceeded to pile each of our dishes with enough meat for five people.

"Oh, I really couldn't finish all this," I protested.

19

"Already you're complaining? You haven't tasted it yet," said Mrs. Tuttman.

"I'm not complaining," I explained. "I just happen to have a small appetite."

"The only cure for a poor appetite is food." And with those words of wisdom, Mrs. Tuttman exited through her swinging doors.

Herman and his father dug into the roast beef, while I kept my eyes glued anxiously on those damn doors. In a few seconds they swung open again and Mrs. Tuttman reentered with a platter of roast chicken.

"Roast beef *and* chicken?" The words escaped my lips before I could stop them. The three Tuttmans seemed somewhat surprised by my remark.

"We *always* have two meats," Herman said condescendingly.

"Nothing is too good for my family," Mrs. Tuttman said with dignity as she placed the equivalent of half a chicken on my plate.

I took a few cautious mouthfuls of meat as Mrs. Tuttman returned to the kitchen. She was back in a flash, scooping mounds of fluffy white potatoes onto everyone's plate.

I began to get nervous. If I overeat, I thought to myself, I'll get sleepy; if I get sleepy, I won't be able to concentrate on the pig; if I don't concentrate, I'll fail the exam; if I fail the exam, I won't become a doctor. This meal could destroy my whole future.

Mrs. Tuttman's kosher catering service was just getting started. There followed, in quick succession, an array of dishes worthy of a bar mitzvah. Cute little saucers of green beans and carrots and bowls of salad

20

now covered every spare inch of table space. The last entry was a plate of knishes. ("Just a side-dish," explained Mrs. T. "Something to fill in the gaps.")

I lost my appetite just looking at all that food, but protesting didn't do any good. Mrs. Tuttman kept heaping food on my plate, and, following the overriding rule of my own household, I felt obligated to finish everything I was served. I slipped some of my knish into my napkin, but that didn't even dent the mountain of food sitting in front of me. My napkin no longer serviceable, I considered slipping food down my sleeves. Too messy and too risky, I decided. I had no alternative but to stuff myself.

Meanwhile, Herman and his father were wolfing food at an incredible rate. Where are they putting it all, I wondered. I purposely dropped my fork in order to get a glance at the floor under the table. Nothing there. They must be eating it, I concluded. Apparently, the Tuttman men had built up a powerful resistance to indigestion in twenty-odd years of being force fed by Mrs. Tuttman.

"What's for dessert?" Herman asked as he swallowed his last mouthful of seconds.

I stifled a moan. I was almost finished with my first round and I felt so bloated I was afraid I would explode at any moment.

"Don't be in such a rush, Herman," Mrs. Tuttman replied. "Lloyd hasn't had seconds yet."

"Oh no. I couldn't," I protested frantically.

"What's wrong? Don't you like my dinner?" Mrs. Tuttman looked deeply offended.

"It was great. It really was, but I ate too much. I'm full."

"I'm not going to force you, Lloyd," she said. "I just hope you don't treat your mother like this. A mother slaves all day over a stove; the only reward she asks is that her family eat and enjoy. But, if making me happy means making you unhappy, then of course I won't press you to have seconds."

With that she turned and left the room, leaving me in an agony of guilt over my inability to eating. Within seconds, however, she retu huge honey-nut cake. Under pressure of her recent attack, I defied the laws of physiology and forced down the generous portion of honey cake she gave me. Fortunately, Herman and his father finished the rest and I didn't have to refuse seconds.

By the time Herman and I descended to the basement where the fetal pig was lying solemnly on a stainless steel tray, I had an acute case of indigestion. Normally, I found kosher food in moderate doses very appealing. However, eating gefilte fish and then facing a fetal pig one-on-one was a great deal to ask. Eating gefilte fish with matza ball soup with roast beef with chicken with green beans with carrots with salad with knish with honey cake and *then* facing a fetal pig one-on-one was going to be an impossible feat. Nonetheless, I was determined to concentrate on studying.

"What's this, Herman?"

"His liver."

I cringed as the strong odor of formaldehyde wafted through the air.

"What's this?" I repeated, pointing at another piggy structure.

"The salivary glands," said Herman, sticking a pin in the salivary glands.

"And this?" I pursued.

"Haven't you studied at all, you ass?"

"There," I pointed triumphantly.

"There what?" snapped Herman, visibly irri-
ta̲t̲e̲

"There s ..e ass. I got one right. I feel sick."

By now my eyes were tearing badly, but Herman was unr°ᵃⁿᵗⁱⁿᵘᵉ This merely added to my nausea. Not only was̲ⁱⁿᵍ ᵃ ⁱ ᵃ ᵃ ᵃune to formaldehyde, he always seemed to know m... e than I. Why? I studied just as hard, but when it came to the test Herman always came out ahead. This didn't do much for my self-confidence and merely served to strengthen my dependence on Herman. He was my human study guide. I realized this dependence was unhealthy, but each time another exam approached my determination to study on my own vanished with my self-confidence. Somehow, I had to break the vicious cycle.

Herman and I studied until four in the morning. I knew that pig inside and out by the time Herman shuffled off to bed and I sacked out on the old couch in his basement. However, I was certain I would forget everything as soon as the exam started.

When I opened my eyes it was morning and, according to my watch, I had fifteen minutes to get to class for the lab exam. Somehow, Herman had neglected to wake me before he left for school.

I rushed up the steps to the door.

"There's freshly-squeezed orange juice and bagels and lox for breakfast," said Mrs. Tuttman, blocking the doorway.

"No! I'm going to be late for the test! Don't you understand?"

"You can't take a big important test on an empty stomach," she protested. "I got up an hour early just so you wouldn't go hungry."

"I've gotta go. You want me to be a doctor, don't you?"

"It would be nice," Mrs. Tuttman smiled, folding her arms. "You and Herman, doctors together."

I politely picked her up and placed her to one side of the door, promising to have bagels and lox another time. I made it to class one minute early. I used that one minute wisely—blasting Herman for forgetting me in the basement. Then I turned my attention to the trays of specimens in the room. I'll never be a doctor, I thought as I winced at the putrid odor of formaldehyde that filled the air.

Promptly at 8:40 a.m., Dr. Sweeney entered the room and all of us scrambled to a station with the answer sheets clutched in our hands. Laboratory examinations were unpleasant and embarrassing. There were forty students and forty stations, each station containing a partially dissected biological specimen ranging from flatworms to fetal pigs to stray cats. Each specimen had a toothpick stuck in a certain organ, muscle, or nerve.

Dr. Sweeney started his alarm clock that would go off every two minutes. Two minutes was the length of time we had to identify the toothpicked part of the specimen in front of us. During those two minutes, which seemed more like two seconds, each student, terrified and panicky, would pick up the specimen and examine it from every conceivable angle, trying desperately to think of the proper descriptive term. At the

24

sound of the alarm, the forty students would simultaneously rotate to the next station. It was kind of like musical bodies.

With me the pattern was predictable. I would start to feel confident about five seconds before the alarm sounded. Then some pushy bastard to the left of me would say, "Time to move, Goldman, let's go," and some turtle to the right of me would mutter, "Stop shoving me, Goldman, you pushy bastard." Then came Dr. Sweeney's voice, "Move along to the station on your right." I would inevitably end up scribbling down a guess.

My fifteenth station on that particular test was a microscopic slide. As usual, the lens was dirty and it was out of focus. There was a large thumbprint on the lens right over the specimen.

"Hell," I muttered.

"What, Mr. Goldman?" Dr. Sweeney was right next to me.

"Nothing, sir."

"No talking. You know better than that." And he walked away with his withered little hands inside his laboratory coat while I read the instructions taped to the desk: Name the green object in the microscopic field. My pulse jumped twenty beats. I was red-green color-blind. I raised my hand. Ten seconds gone. He finally saw me and inched towards my desk. Fifteen more seconds gone.

"Dr. Sweeney, I can't see green. I'm color-blind," I whimpered. Ten more seconds.

"It's the object next to the red cell," he pointed out.

25

"Yes sir, but I can't see red either!" I shrieked.

Twenty seconds more. "Just look hard. By the way, Goldman, what colors *do* you see? Color-blindness could be a serious handicap for any physician."

I wasn't listening to him. I was squinting as hard as I could, trying to see the green thing next to the red cell. It must be a parasite, I concluded, since it was sitting so close to that red cell. I jotted down my answer with confidence and even smirked a little as I scurried to the next station.

I was completely confused by the time I got to the end of the row of stations. I couldn't find the twentieth station and the bell had already begun to ring.

"Hey, Goldman," someone yelled. "Put the frog down." I had been carrying it around with me from the last station. Using one of its rubbery legs as a handle, I sheepishly handed it to the guy who now stood at my last station.

"Where do I go?" I whined.

I noticed an empty station in front and I had just thirty seconds to get there, identify the specimen, and move on. Somehow I did it. That particular frog was exposing a toothpicked parotid gland. "I know that one," I chuckled, thinking of Herman Tuttman and his amazing resistance to formaldehyde fumes. Eventually the fortieth bell rang, and I felt like Noah after the flood.

"Shit," I mused as I walked out of the room, seriously doubting if that's what Noah had said after the flood.

I saw Herman lumbering towards the water fountain. Before I could escape, he spotted me. "Hey, Lloyd, easy test, huh?"

"Sure, Herman. Where are you going?" I was trying to change the subject to keep from getting depressed.

"I need some water." Herman looked pale.

"You feel OK?" I asked, pretending to be concerned. Serves him right, I thought to myself.

"No, Lloyd, I feel kind of lousy. You were right."

"What do you mean? When was I right?"

"About the formaldehyde. All those organs and muscles and little bodies in there. The odor kind of got to me."

I turned away, chuckling to myself.

5

My first year of college was over, but I still had a whole month to worry about my grades in Biology 112. I spent a good part of that month kicking myself in the pants for wasting precious "study" hours trying to convince Cheryl Seltzer to go out with me, for relying too heavily on Herman, and for changing answers from right to wrong during the lab sessions.

So what if I get a C in Biology, I would tell myself. If I don't get into med school, it'll be their loss and not mine. This thought would placate me for a while until Grandmother Schlessel would introduce me as Dr. Goldman or Mrs. Seltzer would inquire about my field of specialization. Then my outlook would change. I'll just kill myself if I don't get that B, that's all. Nice, quick, and simple. I'll lock myself in a room, douse myself with formaldehyde, and die of my own odor.

During this time, I had a chance for a summer job with the Institute of Experimental Biology. I looked forward to this opportunity to get better acquainted with medicine. I would be surrounded by intelligentsia: a Ph.D. in biochemistry, a chemist working on his master's at night, and a biology professor. Even more impressive was the fact that the building I was to work in, all ten stories of it, was dedicated to finding a cure for cancer. It seemed that the sky was the limit.

29

I arranged the following schedule for myself: Every day would be spent in research. Every night, I would search the library files for all possible traces of applicable medical literature. Then, before bed, I would study all the relevant material and formulate revolutionary theories, one of which was bound to be the cure for cancer.

Being a realist, I knew I couldn't come up with an overnight cure, but after all I had sixty nights of summer vacation. I felt sure that if I was on the verge of the answer to cancer, City U. would let me skip the first week or so of school. I was excited about the vast potentialities of my summer job, so excited that I spent the evening before my first day of work rereading *The Double Helix* from cover to cover and inserting "Goldman" in place of the name "Watson."

Next morning, I awoke fifteen minutes before the alarm clock rang while visions of the Nobel Prize were still fogging my brain. I stumbled out of bed, reflecting on every move I made, knowing that some day I would be called upon to recount that "first day" before the American Cancer Society.

When I drove up to the office building on Chevy Chase Lane in Chevy Chase, a little blue-uniformed man opened the door of my car. I approached the entrance and another little blue fellow opened the door to the building. To me, their courteous attention seemed the proper respect due to a man involved in important medical research. I stepped inside and was immediately blasted by the scent of laboratory animals. My ego withered like a ruptured spleen as I began to inhale reminders of Sweeney's lab exam. I turned around in the hallway and went back outside for some fresh air.

All the inhaling and exhaling in the world couldn't help me now—I had stepped down from the American Cancer Society lectern and become just a first-year premed in anguish over a biology grade. After a few deep breaths, I opened the door (this time without the help of the blue men) and walked back into the antiseptic hallway.

"Where is the personnel office, sir?" I asked a guard.

"Three doors down the corrider to your right."

"Thank you."

When I reached the office labeled "Research Personnel" I rang the outside buzzer, straightened my tie, and slipped inside. As I glanced at the receptionist, the introductory speech I had prepared the night before vanished from my memory.

"Oh shit!" I muttered.

"What was that? Oh! Dr. Goldman. Come in. Come in. Cheryl and I are dying to know how you did this year."

There must be thousands of other jobs for college students in Washington, I thought. I don't have to work here.

Mrs. Seltzer was sitting behind a large desk covered with snapshots of her daughter Cheryl, taken from every conceivably decent angle.

"I didn't know that you worked here . . ."

"Oh, I've worked with Irvy for years! You don't think you could have gotten your job without *my* influence do you?"

Irvy? I hope he doesn't ask me to call him that, I thought, ignoring Mrs. Seltzer's attempt to claim my new position as her own accomplishment.

"By the way, Dr. Lloyd, I've got a specialty for you—cardiology. You know—heart-doctoring. Everybody's got chest pains at one time or another. Just the other day my brother Sam thought he was dying of heart failure. Everytime he climbed the steps at home he had an awful sharp pain right over his heart. He was scared to death and I know he would have given his life's savings for a good heart doctor. But you know, Lloyd, he couldn't get an appointment with a specialist for three weeks. He might die by then. Honey, you really should consider specializing. You will live a comfortable life. You'll have it made."

"I haven't made up my mind yet. I've got a long way to go," I replied.

"Lloyd," she continued, experimenting with a new line of attack, "I hear you've been dating gentile girls. Gracious me! Now, Lloyd, why don't you keep to your own kind? I mean how would you raise your children? It would just kill your grandmother. She loves Cheryl. They met the other day, you know. Cheryl and I would love to have lunch with you this afternoon."

Lunch? If I listened to Mrs. Seltzer for one more minute, I'd lose my job and I wouldn't have to worry about lunch. I slowly backed out of the office unnoticed by Mrs. Seltzer, who was still chattering.

I was in the elevator between the third and fourth floors when her voice finally died away. So what, I thought. I'll be so busy researching, studying, formulating, learning, and writing my Nobel Prize speech that I won't even see Mrs. Seltzer. I managed to collect myself in time to comb my hair and check my fly before entering room 415E. Each step across the spotless,

32

sterile, white-tiled hallway was bringing me closer to my big opportunity—the cure for cancer. As my heels hit the hard-surfaced floor, I yearned for a red carpet.

I entered the double glass doors expecting at least one doctor on hand to welcome me. I found myself in a larger-than-life replica of Dr. Sweeney's bio lab. From somewhere among the trays of specimens and the reek of formaldehyde came a voice: "You're late, Goldman."

Late? That's a fine greeting, I thought. How could I be late for my first day? It was Mrs. Seltzer's fault. Her surprise presence at the desk on the first floor had shaken me up.

"I'm sorry," I said to the mustachioed doctor who emerged from behind a tier of small wire cages. "I had a little trouble finding the right place."

"Your instructions are on the bulletin board," he said, walking away.

I stood in front of the bulletin board for about ten minutes, maybe longer. I shook my head. Mice? How was I ever supposed to find the answer to cancer playing with mice. Worse than that, my instructions mentioned nothing about cancer research:

DAILY ROUTINE
1. Weigh mice in cages A through K.
   8:00–10:00 a.m.
2. Tag morning animal shipment and distribute species to proper cages.   10:00–12:30 p.m.
3. Weigh mice in cages L through W.
   1:00–3:00 p.m.
4. Tag afternoon animal shipment and distribute species to proper cages.   3:00–4:30 p.m.

33

I read these directions over three times. Again I stepped down from the American Cancer Society lectern and became a first year premed student or worse—a mouse dispenser.

After three weeks on the job I was eager for anything in the medical research field that did not involve the rodent family. Every time I'd reach into those tiny little cages I would experience two or three annoying bites before I could get the little beast to the weighing scale.

Even listening to Mrs. Seltzer was more desirable than weighing mice. Cheryl was working for the summer in an adjacent office building and Mrs. Seltzer would often bring her along to our luncheons. I found myself phoning Mrs. Seltzer for lunch almost every day.

Cheryl loved her mother and laughed frequently, for no apparent reason, at things her mother said. This giggling invariably caused certain parts of Cheryl's anatomy to convulse sensuously under the tight-fitting sweater she would invariably wear to the cafeteria. So it was worth it to listen to her mother as long as I could watch Cheryl's wonderful breasts juggle around.

"Tell us about your new summer job, Lloyd," Mrs. Seltzer said at one of our first luncheons. "Dr. Silverstein is a real honey, isn't he? Every summer he gives some premed a chance to get acquainted with medicine."

Cheryl motioned to me that I had something on my neck and I wiped off some more meat and potatoes that Mrs. Seltzer had inadvertently sprayed in my direction.

"Unfortunately, the boy who had your job last year quit. His mother got sick or something. As a matter of fact, all the boys who have worked here for the last three summers have had to leave for some reason. It's too bad—they used to really enjoy having lunch with Cheryl and me." Cheryl started giggling. "Of course, they still date Cheryl now and then."

Cheryl giggled harder, and her breasts vibrated.

Mrs. Seltzer continued. "All of the young doctors seem to know how hard it is to find a nice girl with decent morals."

Now Cheryl was trying hard not to laugh and I was trying hard not to ask her why she was laughing.

"My husband and I," continued Mrs. Seltzer with a fork in her mouth, "have devoted our whole lives to raising Cheryl with the highest of moral standards."

What a waste of time, I thought.

"Cheryl knows the difference between right and wrong," asserted Mrs. Seltzer. At this, a soft warm hand began to rub against my thigh, and I knew it wasn't Mrs. Seltzer's. I could feel Cheryl climbing up my leg beneath the table.

"Raising a young lady in this society is no easy job, Doctor. When Cheryl was just five years old she asked Leo and me the old stork question. We spent nearly a week in the library looking up all the current literature on the subject. We also talked to a rabbi, a pediatrician, a gynecologist, and Leo's psychoanalyst. Oh, how we worried. We were so afraid of saying the wrong thing. Thank goodness our efforts have paid off. I'm sure that Cheryl's husband, when she gets married that is, will appreciate our troubles to educate Cheryl on that subject."

I decided she wouldn't have to wait that long to be appreciated; I wanted to appreciate her right now. Cheryl's hand was creeping up and down my leg and each rotation excited me even more. Her sweater seemed to be shrinking and I couldn't stand it any longer. To put it mildly, I was pleasantly surprised by this sudden turn of events. Cheryl pretended to concentrate on her salad while I went crazy.

Finally I jumped up from the table. "Sure nice having lunch with you. Uh . . . you're absolutely right about Cheryl, Mrs. Seltzer. She's definitely the product of your efforts."

"Well, thank you, Dr. Goldman. "You know . . ."

"Cheryl, how about a movie tonight?" I broke in, noticing that Mrs. Seltzer kept right on talking.

Cheryl smiled and I assumed that she wanted a movie.

"See you at eight, ok?" I rushed off to the men's room to wash the succotash off my neck before returning to the mice.

6

I could hardly wait for eight o'clock. That night at the Seltzers, when Cheryl finally wiggled into the room, I began to drool in a somewhat heathen fashion. The first thing I noticed about Cheryl was a very sensuous smile. The next thing I noticed was the deep v-e-e-e of her neckline. She had on a short skirt and my eyes traveled from V-neck to hemline and back again.

"We'd better go. We're late for the movie," I lied.

As we got into the car, I decided against a movie. Not enough privacy. I told myself my intentions were no different than those of any other healthy twenty-one-year-old American boy—I was viciously, desperately, frantically trying to find a warm body on which to expend my sex drives.

"Hey Cheryl, we're going to miss the beginning of this flick. Let's try something else," I said.

"Sure," she cooed without hesitation.

"How about a pizza?" I offered.

"I'm not hungry but I'll watch you eat."

That was a good line. I interpreted it to mean that she didn't care about movies or food.

"Well, what would *you* like to do?" I asked, trying not to be obvious. She unbuckled her seat belt and slid closer to me.

"Maybe a game of golf?" I suggested.

She cuddled up to me and put her head on my shoulder.

"Bowling?"

She began nibbling on my right ear.

"Ice skating? Skeet shooting?"

She subtly unbuckled my seat belt.

"Let's get some wine and cheese and climb Sugar Loaf Mountain," I panted. That sounded like the words to a song.

She blew "Good idea!" into my ear.

It was glorious. I forgot all about my summer misfortunes. I forgot about Mrs. Seltzer and the mice and even my biology grade. I put my arm around Cheryl and headed toward Sugar Loaf Mountain. However, Cheryl's nibbling became more and more aggressive and I decided that it was going to be impossible to wait thirty miles for the mountain.

"How about the Northeast Drive Inn?"

"Good idea," Cheryl whispered again.

I attempted an instant U-turn over an asphalt median strip that sent both of us bouncing around in the car like puppets. Cheryl had been nibbling ferociously at the time and had almost taken my earlobe right off my head.

"Sorry about that bump, baby," I apologized as Cheryl wiped some blood off my collar with my handkerchief. I was convinced that part of my ear had been ripped off and I understood why all my predecessors had quit their summer jobs—they were too ashamed to come to work without earlobes. Cheryl had resumed chewing on my ear now, and I redirected my car towards the Northeast Drive Inn. Meanwhile, Cheryl was running her hand up and down my leg again. There were goose pimples all over my body.

"Lloyd, you've got goose pimples on the palms of your hands," marveled my date.

"I know. I better keep both hands on the wheel. How'd you like to roast some marshmallows at my place?"

"Is there a fire?" Cheryl asked.

What a line! "Sure, there's a nice fireplace and we'll be all alone."

Cheryl giggled and I stopped the car suddenly, backed into a driveway, and headed off in another direction as some poor driver went off the road trying to avoid the rear end of my car. Only eight blocks, I thought, chuckling at my good fortune in having such a voluptuous specimen to examine.

Suddenly, my attention was drawn to a red flashing light which had appeared in my rearview mirror. A closer look showed me that the light was attached to a police car following close behind me. I pulled over to the side of the road as scenes from the past twenty minutes of my joy ride flashed through my mind.

"Lloyd, it's a policeman," Cheryl giggled.

A six-foot-two, blue-uniformed Mr. America emerged from the patrol car and swaggered up to my car.

"I've been following you for quite a while, son, and I'm giving you a ticket. You're drunk."

"No, I'm not . . . Sir," I protested.

"Spell intoxicated," he demanded.

Cheryl giggled and started to recite, "I-n-t-o . . ."

"Shut up, Cheryl," I hissed, fearing she would offend the policeman. However, he seemed highly amused by her witticism. Keeping one eye glued to Cheryl, he made me walk a heel-to-toe straight line. Of course I passed his test without difficulty, except that I was trembling with fear.

"Oh, I see," he said, winking at Cheryl, "you're on drugs."

"D-r-u-g-s," she intoned. They both started to laugh, while I smoldered in anger. I wondered how Cheryl could be so gorgeous and so heartless at the same time and how I could want her so badly. The cop knew where we were going, that was it. Her mother must have told him to follow us.

"Do you know a Mrs. Seltzer?" I demanded, interrupting their tête-à-tête.

"That's my mother!" beamed Cheryl.

"No, son. That won't help you any. I'll drop this little lady off at her house and then you'll have to follow me down to the station."

Cheryl hopped out of the car without even kissing me goodbye. "Call me tomorrow, Lloyd," she said with a wave of the hand. I climbed back into my car and began to follow the patrol car. My worst fears were realized as I watched Cheryl gradually inch across the front seat until she blended with Mr. Six-foot-two behind the wheel.

I never got to the police station that night. When the patrol car started heading away from the city in the direction of Lovers' Lane, I turned toward home.

40

7

During the last week in June, I ate lunch at home. The mail was delivered between twelve and one at our house and my grades were on the way. Every lunch hour, I'd sit staring blankly at the mail slot on the front door until I heard the footsteps of the mailman outside. I'd catch all the letters, advertisements, circulars, and magazines before they hit the floor. If there was no correspondence from City University, I would dash outside after the postman and accuse him of withholding mail in transit, a federal offense. After about four days he caught on and learned to ignore me as I ranted and raved, following behind him along his route. I think he actually enjoyed watching my delirium.

On the fifth day of the last week of June, I was in position as usual when the mail fell through the slot. I caught it, sorted it as usual, and dashed outside screaming at the mailman.

"It's not here. It's gotta be here. Herman got his yesterday! Where's mine?" I cried.

"Where's your what?" the postman asked innocently.

"My grades! You know."

"No, I'm afraid not." He began to smile so I knew he was lying. "I delivered something from your college though."

41

"Where is it? I didn't see it." I began sifting through the mail again to double-check. "You're lying. There's nothing here."

The mailman started checking in his mailbag and going through the neighbor's mail to make sure. "You're Goldman, aren't you?"

"Of course I'm Goldman. And I'm expecting a little envelope from City University."

"That's why you've been yelling at me all week?" he asked.

"Yes, Yes. Check your bag again. I need those grades."

The postman turned on his heel and started to walk down the sidewalk. I dropped all my parents' mail and started following him.

"Look, Goldman," he sighed, still walking, "I delivered your grades today. Check your mail again. It's in there somewhere. Look in between the pages of one of your magazines."

I raced back to where I'd dropped all the mail and looked through the *National Geographic*. Nothing. I went through *Time*, page by page. Nothing there either. By now I was kneeling in the middle of the sidewalk in broad daylight and a crowd was gathering.

"What are you looking for?" asked a middle-aged woman.

"Here," I grumbled, handing her the *Reader's Digest*, "thumb through this. I'm looking for a letter from City University."

I picked up a *Ladies' Home Journal* and shook it.

"There!" cried a little boy whose face was stuck to

a lollipop. As he shouted, a small white envelope fell into the grass by his feet.

"Don't touch that, son," I warned him, motioning the crowd to stand back. "I'll handle this."

I picked up the envelope and read the first line of the address: "To the parents of Lloyd Goldman." The return address was "Registrar, City University."

"This is it!" I screamed, clutching it tightly in my fist and shoving it into my pocket. My crowd was applauding.

I paid the little boy who had spotted my prize a quarter.

"Twenty-five cents?"

"You little squirt," I muttered and handed him another dime.

I gathered up the remains of my family's mail and took it into the house. I noticed that something was missing and ran back outside. The crowd was dispersing.

"Hey, where's the lady with my *Reader's Digest*?"

"Oh, she's gone," said a young man with a briefcase.

"She stole my magazine!"

"Oh, she thought you gave it to her."

I returned to my house and scurried upstairs where I locked myself in my room.

I placed the envelope on my desk and sat down in front of it. Through the small transparent window I reread: "To the parents of Lloyd Goldman." I wondered what that computer would do if it knew I was opening what was technically my parents' mail. I wondered what my parents would do. I couldn't help it; I had suffered long enough. I tore open the envelope.

43

General Chemistry 101	A
Calculus 115	A
English Composition 100	B
Biology 112	B

I breathed easier; a B in biology was like a ticket to heaven. The big hurdle. Gleefully, I read the accompanying letter stating that I had made the Dean's List. My parents wouldn't care that I had opened this letter. They would, however, be disturbed to learn their *Reader's Digest* had been pilfered.

I went into the bathroom and opened the medicine chest. I closed the medicine chest and looked in the mirror. Miraculously, a stethoscope appeared around my neck, and my sweaty T-shirt was transformed into blue surgical garb. I reopened the medicine chest and started pondering over the prospective specialties open to me now that I had proven myself. Surgery? Good money, reasonable hours, considerable respect from the community. Yet I'd always had trouble handling a knife at the dinner table. I decided that I would wait a little while before giving Mrs. Seltzer the satisfaction of a commitment. Instead, I would casually mention my grades and watch her squirm.

I didn't waste any time. Upon my return to work I stopped off at Mrs. Seltzer's desk.

"The Dean's List!" she whistled, suitably impressed. "What grades did you make Lloyd?"

"Two A's and two B's," I said, smirking slightly.

"An A in biology! How wonderful!"

"Uh . . . no, a B in biology. But I got an A in chemistry."

"Lloyd, Lloyd, a B in biology," Mrs. Seltzer shook her head. "You have to know your way around the human body before you can cut on it, Lloyd. I would have liked to see an A."

"Leave me alone!" I cried, and stalked out of the office.

There was no doubt about it. Mrs. Seltzer had a talent for deflating an already shaky ego.

8

It was time for a decision—Cheryl or premed. It was September and I had just begun my second year of college. I knew I couldn't afford to fail anything, even a homework assignment, from now on. Competition for med school was simply too stiff. Cheryl, hardly an intellectual, had no pressing academic demands. I had made some progress since that disastrous summer evening (I guess the 'prestige' of dating a premed, now a *second year* premed had finally gotten to her) and she squeezed me into her social calendar almost once a week, although never on weekends—those were reserved for tall, dark, handsome football types.

In my more rational moments, I told myself I had no choice but to give up pursuing Cheryl. Medical school was an infinitely more worthwhile goal. But, no sooner had I come to this decision than I would change my mind. I wanted Cheryl's body and I was determined to get it.

These thoughts were racking my brain one Saturday afternoon as I sat in the science library trying to concentrate on organic chemistry. The first quiz was Monday, and I didn't want to blow it.

"In heterolytic reactions," I read, "bonds are broken unsymmetrically and electrons remain coupled."

Coupled? Oh no! How is a guy supposed to

concentrate if they put ideas like that in an organic text? It's a conspiracy, that's what it is. Textbook writers are bribed by med school admission panels to help weed out unworthy applicants. Thoughts of my unworthiness, Cheryl and coupled bonds leapt to my mind, but I fought them back.

I continued my reading, concentrating fiercely. I was doing well, until I turned the page and read, "In substitution reactions, single bonds are made and broken at carbon, and a new (incoming) group is substituted for the old."

As if there was a tiny movie projector inside my brain, Cheryl flashed before my eyes. I could see all too clearly what would happen if I decided my studies should come before Cheryl. The tenuous relationship (single bond) we had established would be broken and some other guy (the new incoming group) would be substituted for me (the old).

I was in agony. What could I do? Was the reaction reversible? I read on. I combed that chapter and the next and started over again. The afternoon wore on, and it grew dark outside. I was hovering on the brink of despair when suddenly—a miracle.

"In organic chemistry, many molecules and ions are encountered which are composed of groups of atoms held together by bonds strong enough to preserve themselves under a variety of conditions."

"Then there's hope," I cried aloud. My exclamation was greeted by annoyed glances and *shhh* sounds from students sitting nearby.

My eyes continued devouring the page. "These bonds are composed of *pairs of electrons* simultaneously attracted by the positive charges in the nuclei of the atoms that are bonded. . . . Atoms are often held together by double bonds, and in effect four electrons are shared by two nuclei."

"That's it!" I yelled. "A double bond."

"Will someone throw that idiot out of here?" an irate scholar demanded.

I had the answer. I must strengthen the bond between Cheryl and myself and I knew exactly how to do that—through Mrs. Seltzer. I had contributed one electron—my premed status. Cheryl had contributed another—her body. That was our single bond. Now, enter Mrs. Seltzer into the reaction. The Mrs. Seltzer electrons (her maternal love and her yearning for a medical son-in-law) were simultaneously attracted to daughter Cheryl nucleus and future Dr. Lloyd Goldman nucleus.

In other words, all I had to do was make Mrs. Seltzer think my intentions toward her daughter were both serious and honorable and she would keep my memory alive in Cheryl's mind at least until organic chem was over.

I closed my text; I knew what I must do. It was Saturday night, and Cheryl would be away from home on a date. That meant that Mrs. Seltzer would be up waiting for her darling daughter's return. I gathered my books together and left the library. I climbed into my car, turned the key in the ignition, squared my shoulders and headed for the Seltzer household. . . .

On Monday, I aced my organic quiz.

9

The final three years of undergraduate school sort of puttered along. I stayed out of trouble, kept my grades up, kept my mouth shut, smiled a lot at pedantic professors, and began to have recurring bouts of nausea. The monotony was making me sick, not because I wasn't busy (I was always busy), but because I wasn't doing what I wanted to do. I never did find a cure for cancer and, as Mrs. Seltzer predicted, I quit playing with those mice after one summer.

All college students, especially those pressured by postgraduate requirements, face crises. I was no exception. For example, in my qualitative chemistry course I miscalculated in a simple addition exercise in the middle of a two-hour exam problem. The professor took off full credit, and I failed the exam with a score of zero. Thus began one of my major battles for grades. I spent a full afternoon with Dr. Benson, trying to explain that the concept had been realized, the logical steps had been carried through and all I had done was make one stupid little mistake. I launched into a forty-five minute harangue that left me exhausted and almost put Dr. Benson to sleep.

"Goldman, please," he groaned, "don't try to fight the system with logic."

Before I could puzzle over the subtleties of that

remark, Benson continued, "Goldman, you want to be a doctor, right? Well, a doctor can't afford to make *any* mistakes, no matter how simple. The smallest mistake could result in the loss of a life."

"Dr. Benson," I stammered, for his argument was a blow below the belt, "are you telling me that if I added 265 to 133.7 and got 398.8 someone would die?"

"It's very possible."

"What if I had the theory right, the process right . . ."

"Goldman, you failed the exam."

I spent that evening in my room contemplating Benson's refusal to give me a more lenient grade. The impact of his remarks began to take on philosophical proportions. I was talking about D's and F's, and Benson was talking about life and death. Suppose some day I accidently gave a patient a toxic dose of a drug? Suppose I administered the wrong medication in the middle of a major operation? For the rest of my life, my conscience would be laden with guilt. These thoughts weighed so heavily on my mind that I seriously considered quitting the medical profession. For the first time I began to realize that, as a doctor, I would not be immune to human error.

In retrospect I can see that, although my conflict with Dr. Benson didn't get me a higher grade, it taught me a valuable lesson. An M.D. or a string of Ph.D.'s behind one's name does not exempt anyone from membership in a fallible species of animal: homo sapiens. Doctors make fatal mistakes and embarrassing blunders. When a bricklayer makes a mistake, a wall falls down. When a doctor makes one, someone gets more seriously ill or dies. It happens every day in both cases.

All men learn to live with their mistakes, but I wondered then if I could ever learn to live with the knowledge that my error had cost someone his life. Everyone in the profession must learn to cope with this burden.

I decided that the severity of my math error had not been exaggerated by Dr. Benson and that I would drop the matter.

Another "crisis" in my premed life concerned my attempts to outdistance my professors in their lectures. There was, in undergraduate courses, a tendency on the part of many professors to place an inordinate amount of importance on *how much* material was presented, and not enough on *how well* the students absorbed any of it. These professors spent every lecture session glued to the blackboard chasing a piece of chalk with an eraser, as if both chalk and eraser were controlled by magnetic forces. They tried to squeeze three hours of subject material into one hour of lecture time with no discussion allowed. Most of them wrote and spoke so rapidly that not even the most adroit legal secretary could have kept pace with them. Another annoying habit was their tendency to contradict what they had said five minutes before.

The front row was a cherished place in these classrooms. Grade-grubbers of all types would fight viciously for seats every day and several ugly brawls occurred. The tape recorder contingent was usually the most eager, but when it came to fighting they backed off; they didn't want to wreck their precious machines. There were those few speed readers who brought only a textbook and a magic marker to class, following Dr.

What's-His-Face's lecture topic by topic, heads bobbing up and down with every word. There were a few students who had mastered shorthand. If they couldn't get a front row seat they really didn't mind. They sat in a group wherever they decided to settle, often gloating over some poor slob who was still having trouble writing longhand. Sometimes a business major would sneak into a premed course just for kicks and take notes like a scribe, later having them Xeroxed and sold to clients for a dollar a page.

I tried all of these methods at one time or another. Longhand note-taking was the first. In this endeavor I was seriously hampered by a wandering mind and poor reflexes. There were certain words that would immediately cause me to daydream in the middle of a purely scientific discussion. Words like "sex" and "food" were sure-fire stimuli. If I was in a less conscientious mood, it would take words like "procreate" and "nutrition" to veer my mind off the track. If I was in an exceptionally impressionable mood, following nothing at all the professor was saying, peculiar words like "follicle" or "nostril" would cause my mind to wander.

I decided that a new method of note-taking was needed. Since it would have taken too long to master shorthand, I invested in a tape recorder, convinced it was a foolproof method. I brought the new recorder to class early enough to secure a front row seat and, when the professor began his lecture, I confidently turned it on. Suddenly, the room was filled with the sounds of heavy breathing accompanied by an occasional grunt. I had forgotten to erase an obscene phone call one of my friends had generously allowed me to record the day before in order to test my new recorder. As the class dissolved in laughter, I grabbed the tape recorder and switched it from "play" to "record." Finally, with a look of stern disapproval, the professor resumed lecturing. It was heaven. All I had to do was sit back and relax. After class, I trotted out to my car to listen to my tape.

I turned it on, expecting to hear the explanation of a very difficult chemical formula. Instead, there was silence. I checked to make sure that the recorder was on "play."

Herman was sitting next to me wolfing a salami sandwich.

"What's the matter with this thing?" I cried, frantically. "Look, it's on 'play'." I started shaking the machine.

"Lloyd," said Herman, "you did have it on 'record' during the lecture, didn't you? You did make sure of that?"

"Really, Herman, I do have a brain," I said in my most biting tone as I continued to shake the tape recorder.

"Stop it, you'll break it," said Herman, "give it to me." He examined it for a minute. "Where's the mike?"

"The mike?" My voice cracked.

"The microphone. Plugs in here. Remember? It's the little square thing you talk into so your voice will come out of the magic box. Remember?"

"Shit." I opened the glove compartment, and there was the microphone.

"I guess you can't record very well without the mike, can you?" Herman took another bite of his sandwich.

55

"Herman," I said in my most humble tone, "can I borrow your notes?"

Another time I subscribed to the Xerox wizard's note-taking service. This was equally disastrous. I approached the wizard (a business major, of course) and asked for a copy of the day's notes. In good faith, I prepaid my dollar fee. The next day in my mailbox I found the "copy." It was barely visible, much less legible.

"What the hell is this?" I yelled over the phone. "I can't read this crap!"

"Listen, I just deliver the orders," he explained. "I have nothing to do with how they turn out. I don't even mail them myself. I'm a middleman, Goldman. Leave me alone." He gave me another number to call.

"What the hell is this?" I cried again.

"Are the notes faint?" inquired the copier, politely.

"Faint? That's an understatement. I want one I can read. I need these notes."

The copier promised me a free, legible copy and told me to check my mailbox the next day. He was a man of honor. I did find a legible copy—but of the wrong notes.

"I'm getting a little tired of this," I warned the business major next day in class. "Tell your copier friend to get me the right notes by tomorrow or I'll Xerox his face."

Business majors were insidious but easily frightened. I got the right notes, but it cost me two dollars more. That was my first and last experience with the Xerox wizard. I was back where I started—taking notes in longhand.

Eventually I ended up taking all the notes myself, selling them to no one. I usually learned little, if anything, from professors who assumed that all college students were sponges. I hated them, but they were too busy to hate me back.

"I hate that bastard," I told Herman one day, speaking about the blackboard magnet, Dr. Prescott.

"He doesn't know you're alive," said Herman.

"I know, but I hate him for not knowing I'm alive."

"Raise your hand," said Herman, "He'll know about you then."

Nobody raises a hand during Prescott's lectures; the class started buzzing when I raised mine. Dr. Prescott turned around and glared contemptuously.

"You there," he croaked, "what's your name? What's the matter?"

"I'm Lloyd Goldman, sir. I don't understand that formula."

Prescott turned his back on me. "Ask one of your buddies. Ask Tuttman. He's a smart guy. Ask him after class."

"Herman!" I whispered bitterly, "How does he know *your* name?"

"Later, Lloyd," he replied, suppressing a laugh. "Gotta get these notes."

10

Tens of thousands of them.
On your mark!
All of them as desperate as myself.
Get set!
Swarming the countryside like lemmings.
Go!

All of them trying to get into medical school, trying anything, looking everywhere for a place to take their B.S. degree and bloated ambitions. Every fall another 45,000 unrelenting creatures summon all available resources as they compete for a place in one of the nation's 110 odd medical schools. Fewer than one out of every three will get in.

Anything is fair play in the fight for admission. After you've spent four years busting your ass to keep a B average, you are hardly willing to admit that medicine is not your bag. A recommendation from an uncle who had a cousin who was good friends with an M.D. who had graduated from so-and-so university always helped. Or a reference from a neighbor who used to play cards with a widow whose husband had given large sums of money to the medical library—that would be a plus.

There are other guys who make it because they have mastered only one thing in life—multiple-choice exams. They know the difference between true and

59

false, between all of the above and none of the above and just a few of the above. These fellows go through merit scholarship tests at a mind-boggling pace. They know everything about tests but nothing about life. They are easy to spot: thick glasses, baggy pants, narrow ties, and dandruff. Sometimes, however, they appear in disguise—longer hair and jeans. All admission committees love multiple choice freaks. Ninety-eighth percentile in science, 91st percentile in English composition, and 96th percentile in math—this excites the committee. Some of these students climb social ladders and become rich, successful doctors who can't tie their own shoelaces.

Some med school applicants are mistaken for geniuses because they have mastered the rote memory technique. They have the closest thing to total recall possible, and, like parrots, they repeat verbatim everything they've learned. Maintaining high grades is a snap when you remember every trivial detail in every textbook you've ever read.

If your family is wealthy, you can improve your chances by applying to as many schools as possible. However, at fifteen to twenty-five dollars a shot, the average guy can afford, at the outside, seven applications.

My father wasn't rich, and I had neither photographic memory nor mastery over multiple choice exams, but I joined the herd anyway. I looked all over the United States for a friendly medical school. I sent for twelve catalogs and applied to seven schools.

Then came an agonizing period of waiting to be contacted for interviews. During this trying time, when my resistance was at an all time low, temptation, in the person of Herman Tuttman, entered my life. My true friend had stumbled onto a sure way to get me into med school.

"Goldman, here's the answer to your problem," he proclaimed, handing me a colorful brochure which read:

"Attention perplexed premeds! The following case histories are true:

"Case I—Mark was a C student—performed poorly on his med school admission exams with embarrassingly low scores in science and math. Mark was rejected by more than a dozen American medical schools. We found him a spot in five foreign programs!

"Case II—Without a prayer for acceptance into an accredited U.S. medical program, John applied to a score of dental schools. He was rejected by all twenty because he had been arrested for stealing hubcaps as a teenager in his hometown. John sought our help and, within three months, we found him a spot in three foreign programs.

"Case III—Kevin partied in high school, but he squeezed into college. Kevin partied in college, but he squeezed into medical school. Kevin got squeezed out of medical school on his tail. Today, Kevin is partying in a foreign medical school."

These amazing case histories were attractive, but the personalized letter was even more alluring:

Dear Student,

Top Notch Counseling, Ltd. is an organization dedicated to helping those with academic

61

deficiencies find a way. The medical division of our committee of experts has been notified of your shaky status, and we are eager to place you in a foreign institution. *Good Doctors are Needed in Europe, Asia, and Africa!*

Just fill in your name and address on the enclosed prepaid postcard, and follow-up arrangements will be made for an extensive analysis by our medical referral committee. At that time, a list of prospective foreign schools will be issued to you. The fee for these services is $400. Send us a Xerox copy of your college diploma plus another $800, and we will *guarantee* you a place in a foreign school. All these institutions are fully accredited and highly respected, and resident licenses are valid in the U.S. Remember our successful clients—Mark, John, and Kevin. We wish you the best of luck.

Sincerely,
John W. McMichael, Pres.

What Herman had just handed me was Madison Avenue in its most obnoxious form. The whole counseling agency scene turned me off. There were many excellent foreign schools, of course, but these agencies existed because of the shortage of U.S. medical institutions. There were plenty of well-qualified students who didn't get into med school merely because there was not enough room for them. And, instead of creating the room, we were exporting our students and importing thousands of foreign-trained doctors each year in order to ease our country's doctor shortage. In the process, we were ignoring the fact that many foreign countries need the doctors they train.

I didn't like what Herman was offering; however, I also knew the odds against getting into medical school.

"Herman, where can I get a copy of the application?"

"Silverstein."

"I can't go through with it," I said. "I'm an American. I can't pay my way to success. I've got to *prove* that I've got medical ability."

"Come on, Lloyd," scoffed my friend. "Don't give me your phony morality. You're the one who needs a med school."

"How can I get a copy of the application?" Herman was watching me squirm.

"I thought you couldn't go through with it," he taunted.

"I can't! This contradicts everything I've ever believed in."

"Well, OK, just forget I showed you this . . . "

"Herman, please." I whined. "Give me the address."

"I don't have it, Lloyd. Silverstein has it."

"Isn't it on the letter?" I took the papers from his hands and examined them. They had been carefully doctored so that the letterhead had been removed.

"What is this?" I demanded.

"Silverstein," said Herman. "He's afraid that if anyone else sees this thing, it'll make foreign med schools more popular than American ones. He's very patriotic."

63

"So am I!" I snapped. "And he's right—this is disgusting. This operation says that anyone with money has a better chance of becoming a doctor. That *is* anti-American!"

"No it isn't," argued Herman. "You need thousands and thousands of dollars to go through U.S. med schools, too."

"That's beside the point," I countered weakly. "Will Silverstein give me the address?"

"Are you kidding?" laughed Herman.

"Oh well, I guess I'll have to sweat it out. By the way, why did he give *you* the letter? Who the hell are you?"

"He gave it to *me* because *I've* already been accepted at the school *I* want. He thought I would get a chuckle out of it."

"Herman, for God's sake. Don't play these stupid games. Why did he take the letterhead off if he knew you'd been accepted?"

"I'm not sure, Lloyd, but as he ripped it off he told me to show the letter to you. He thought you might get a kick out of it."

"Herman, is there any way I can get that address? I mean just in case. After all, my future is at stake here."

"Yeah. There's one way. Silverstein has got this secretary that is willing to release the address to anyone within earshot. Her name is Mrs. . . . . "

"Seltzer!" I choked.

"How'd you know?"

"Never mind," I mumbled. If Mrs. Seltzer was in

this, I *knew* I didn't want any part of it. "Like I said, I wouldn't think of applying outside the country. . . . " I continued talking until I had finally convinced myself that, as long as there was still a chance for a domestic medical education, I was going to try.

11

High school, college, med school, residency, specialization . . . a nice Jewish boy who aspires to become a nice Jewish doctor faces a lifetime of competition, stress, and hard work. The interview, a prerequisite for admission to medical school, can bring the metamorphosis to a grinding halt. In the brief span of an hour, a lifelong dream may be shattered. The admission interview is one of the most torturous experiences I have ever endured.

I had spent several months rehearsing—nay, perfecting—what I felt would be the most important role of my life.

"Gentlemen," I addressed the bathroom mirror, "ever since I was twelve I have sought a meaningful profession. I want to contribute to this great society of ours. I want to help the needy, to heal the sick, to rehabilitate the disabled. I yearn for an education which will give me the tools for that mission. Gentlemen, I want to dedicate my life to mankind."

Too godly, said the mirror.

"Gentlemen." I tried again, "I'm honored to be with you today. My own life has been plagued with multiple medical problems. I was stricken with scarlet fever at age five, but, thanks to modern medicine, I pulled through. I was crushed in a bizarre auto accident

67

at the age of ten, but, thanks to modern surgical methods, I was saved. I was bedridden with a deadly case of infectious hepatitis at the age of fifteen, but, again thanks to medical research, I lived. Never will you find one more appreciative of the science of healing. I owe my life to medicine. Please let me give it . . ."

Stop, said the mirror, you're making *me* sick.

My next approach was genetically oriented.

"Gentlemen, doctors grow on my family tree. My great grandfather was the only physician in a small town in Austria. Thousands of the common folk were dependent upon his services. My grandfather worked with Albert Schweitzer in Africa. He dedicated his life to healing the savages. My maternal uncle was a country doctor in the destitute Appalachian areas. Money was of no concern to him. I seek now to uphold this tradition. Please let me bring to fruition the seed of my heritage . . ."

"Ma! Lloyd won't come out of the bathroom! And he's talking to himself in the mirror," yelled my little brother Edward. Edward would always pick the most inappropriate moments to have to go to the bathroom.

In spite of Edward's frequent interruptions, I was confident that I had found the appropriate mixture of humility, pride, gravity, and humor by the time my first interview rolled around. It took place at a medical center on the West Coast. This was in direct opposition to Grandmother Schlessel's wishes. She pleaded with me all the way to the airport not to go, to stay in the East with "parents who love you like a son." She warned of the "evil West," infested with "hippies and venereal disease."

I went anyway.

68

I felt the color drain from my face as I arrived at the appointed room. During the following thirty minutes I was to be evaluated on my performance in college, my scores on the medical boards and admission exams, and my composure in front of the interviewers. Each member of the admission committee would evaluate me individually; hopefully, each would arrive at the same favorable conclusion. The task of each member was to ascertain whether I was worthy of joining the elite medical profession. I took a deep breath, turned the door knob, and walked in. Three stern-faced, gray-haired, cigar-smoking doctors sat at the opposite end of a long, narrow table.

"Sit down, son," said the doctor in the middle. I immediately pegged him as the chairman of this august panel.

I dropped into a chair facing them. I had never seen three meaner looking individuals in my life. They scrutinized me for what seemed like a millenium while my stomach churned in nervous anticipation. Finally, the chairman stood up, walked around the table, and stopped in front of me. He inhaled deeply on the foot-long cigar he had been munching, leaned close to me, and exhaled the fumes directly into my face.

"Why you?" he demanded. "What makes you any more qualified than the other applicants?" No handshake, no hello, no smile. Just the big question.

What I had feared for months now happened—I drew a blank. All those hours of preparation slipped into the twilight zone of my memory. I couldn't recall one phrase, one idea of any of my approaches.

The three cigars were aimed at me like cannons.

The chairman sighed impatiently.

"Well?"

I just sat there.

"Son, surely you must have thought about this. Why do you want to be a doctor? Why *should* you be a doctor?"

"Because," I attempted a smile, "I *want* to."

There was a loud, stereo, simultaneous cough . . . .

Finally the longest half hour in my life drew to a close. When I was dismissed, I ran down the hall as fast as I could go in the direction of the men's room, where I vomited my lunch.

I grabbed the first plane back to Washington. My next problem, having given up on a medical career, was to explain my failure to my family. This was no easy task. Grandmother Schlessel's outspoken confidence in my career plans had left the general impression in our neighborhood and social circle that I was already an M.D.

There was the synagogue scene—on the high holy days we'd stand outside the temple hand in hand:

"I'd like you to meet my grandson, the doctor."

There were the lively weddings and bar mitzvahs. We'd stand in the reception line:

"Honey, glad to see you. I'd like to introduce my grandson, Dr. Lloyd Goldman."

I decided all this was finished. As soon as I debarked from the plane, I would lay it on the line. Number one, I'm not a doctor; and, number two, I screwed up my first interview for med school.

I stepped from the airplane to see my welcoming party gathered below—Grandmother Schlessel, Mom, and Dad.

"I won't let them have you," said Grandmother as soon as I was within earshot. "We need good doctors in the East."

Amid all the handshaking and hugging I was bravely trying to admit defeat. "I've got something to tell all of you. I . . ."

"Lloyd," said Grandmother, "when I die, I want *you* to do the autopsy. A stranger? Never!"

"But I have to tell you what happened today . . ."

"Lloyd, we're proud of you," said my father gruffly. "This is a big decision, a decision that must be your very own."

My mother nodded her head in agreement.

"But as for me," he continued, "I'd love to see you stay right here in Washington."

Unable to face my father, I turned to my grandmother again. "Listen, please! The interview was a complete . . ."

"The girls are not pure in the West, are they, Lloyd?" she said before I could open my mouth.

"Son," my father said, "medicine is a fine profession and you've made the big decision to study it. It is now time to make another decision, to make another move in the chess game of life."

"My pawns have been wiped out," I mumbled. No one heard me. "If you would just be quiet, I could tell you what happened!"

"Lloyd, welcome home!" Mother, who had been silent until now, took a box wrapped in gold paper from behind her back.

I unwrapped the gift hesitantly.

"O-o-o-o-h!" cooed Grandmother. "Well, Doctor, you're all set now. Congratulations!"

71

It was a District of Columbia M.D. license tag clearly labeled with my projected date of graduation—my family's plans for my future, summed up neatly on a license tag!

"Thanks. It's very . . . impressive," I mumbled.

"Your father knows the head of the Department of Motor Vehicles and he had it arranged just for you," said my mother.

I gave up trying to explain what had happened and resigned myself to enduring the remaining interviews for the sake of my family.

Somehow, I learned to live with the humiliation of that first interview. I had six more and with each one I became more practiced in some respects, but less sure of myself in others. Invariably, as soon as my confidence would begin to grow, some remark or incident would summon my usual feelings of inadequacy.

There was the interview at a midwestern school where I had the opportunity to meet some of my competitors. A group of us were given a tour of the campus and a luncheon after which we were scheduled for individual interviews.

We were a motley crew. The most peculiar was a guy with acne, braces, narrow tie, baggy pants, fly half way down—the whole bit. There was another of the same type—only a girl. At the other extreme was the fraternity jock—crew cut, muscular build, and black spit-shined shoes with tacks in the heels that clicked in a military fashion when he walked.

I felt a surge of self-confidence as I sized up my competitors. Well at least I've got the advantage over these losers in appearance, I thought to myself.

"Excuse me," said a voice at my elbow. It was the female loser. "Do you set your hair? I wish I could get my hair to look so wild and woolly."

If that blow were not enough to deflate my ego, the conversation which followed was. Acne casually mentioned his credentials.

"You jokers don't stand a chance," he sneered. "I've already had a paper published on an independent research project in cytology."

"How quaint. I have a master's in pathology," replied his female counterpart.

"My father is on the board of trustees," grinned the jock. Even Acne was overwhelmed by this bit of information.

"I've done cancer research in the Institute of Experimental Biology," I said, wondering how a few weeks of playing with mice would stack up before an admissions panel when compared to the accomplishments (and connections) of my three competitors. I was only beginning to understand the kind of competition I was up against.

Another interview took place at a medical center in the Northeast. I felt I had established a rapport with my judges and had answered their questions intelligently. Two weeks after the interview I received my rejection notice in the mail.

Eventually, I was accepted to two schools. Against the wishes of my family, I chose to attend a medical center in Chicago. To this day, I do not know what I said or did at those two interviews that made the difference. But I was in, and that's all that mattered. Now I could go on competing, striving, and working my fingers to the bone.

12

"Now, have you got that?" My mother's muffled voice was coming from my closet. "You can wear number 'three' socks with number 'one' shirt and sweater but not vice versa. And the 'two' shirt goes with 'two,' 'three,' and 'four' pants. That should just about do it for your *winter* wardrobe."

" 'Three' with 'one,' 'two' with . . . um . . . why don't I write that down?" My head was spinning.

"Lloyd, how do you expect to become a doctor if you can't remember a few simple numbers?"

"A few simple numbers?" I cried. "I'll need a computer to help me get dressed every morning."

It was the day before I was to leave home for med school, and I was getting my first glimpse of how perilous life away from the security and stability of my family would be. For twenty-two color-blind years, my mother had been my insurance against social gaucherie. Not once had she let me leave the house mismatched. When powder blue with kelly green was simply unheard of, my mother took every precaution against the possibility of my creating such an unlucky combination. The very next season, when the same color coordinates became the rage, she spared no effort including them in my wardrobe.

Now I would be on my own. What if I chose a red shirt to wear with my burgundy pants? Worse yet, what if my socks didn't match? I would never live it down.

"Don't look at me like that, Lloyd. I'll go get a piece of paper and a pen if it will make you feel better," relented my mother.

She left the room and I continued numbering my new socks with a laundry marker. This, I was sure, would prevent any mix-up. I was being especially careful and was thoroughly engrossed by my work when suddenly my eardrums were shattered.

"Oh, isn't that cute?! He's numbering his socks!"

It was Mrs. Seltzer and, of course, Cheryl. As usual, both were laughing at my expense.

"How did you get in?" I demanded, my face aflame.

"We happened to be in the neighborhood shopping and we wanted to say goodbye. Your mother told us we'd find you up here."

My mother had no sense of privacy.

"I know you're just sick about having to leave home," continued Mrs. Seltzer, "but don't feel so bad, honey. One day you'll be a rich and successful and famous doctor in our community. I made it perfectly clear to Dean Roland that he will be very sorry he didn't accept you."

"*You* spoke to Dean Roland?" I asked. Dr. Roland was the dean of a local medical center I had applied to. Apparently Mrs. Seltzer hadn't taken the news of my imminent departure too well. I hated Dean Roland when I was rejected, but now I pitied him. In my wildest fantasies of revenge, I had never imagined anything so cruel as sending Mrs. Seltzer to "reason" with him.

"It wasn't his fault," I defended Dean Roland, "there was a whole committee who decided."

"Oh, really?" Mrs. Seltzer's eyes narrowed. "Do you have their names? Maybe it's not too late. I could pay them a visit . . ."

"No!" I shouted. "I mean—that's all right," I added in a calmer voice. "It's over and done and I've made up my mind to leave. It'll be tough, but I'll work hard and the time will go by very quickly."

"Cheryl and I don't know what we're going to do without our little doctor around, do we Cheryl?"

Cheryl had wandered into my closet. I could see her examining my pink shirt. She seemed fascinated by the big number "one" my mother had written on the inside of the collar.

"What?" she said, momentarily coming out of the fog. "Oh, sure, Lloyd." I could see she was overcome by emotion at the mere mention of my departure.

"Well, thank you for coming by."

I ushered them toward the door.

"It was a nice thought."

I opened the door.

"Cheryl's got something to show you, Lloyd."

I shut the door.

Reaching into a little shopping bag, Cheryl removed two slivers of baby-blue cloth and blushed.

"Show him, honey. Show the doctor," coached her mother with a sly smile.

Cheryl held one of the slivers up over her breasts. "See, it goes like this."

Aha! A bikini! My imagination began to see, all too clearly, Cheryl barely covered, barely decent, barely. Not content with attacking the dean, Mrs. Seltzer was now going to work on me.

"Sit down, folks," I offered. "Would you like something to eat? I don't have to pack for a while and this *will* be the last time we have a chance to chat."

"And the bottom piece goes like this," said Mrs. Seltzer, stretching the cloth across Cheryl's pelvis. "Do you like the color, Lloyd?"

"It's fine," I said, watching Cheryl struggle with her mother in an attempt to get the bikini back into the bag.

"Why don't you put it on for the doctor? Lloyd, you don't mind, do you? You've got time. Hurry up, honey, go slip it on for Lloyd."

I sank into a chair and crossed my legs. Cheryl slinked out of the room, and I began to wonder if she were in on this or if she were merely an instrument of her mother's deranged vengeance.

"Cheryl is such a darling," Mrs. Seltzer continued. "She's going to make someone a fine wife. Once she gets to know someone, she'll do anything for them!"

"Anything?" I mused.

"Take her father . . . Cheryl gives him a back rub every single day after he gets home from work. She brings him his newspaper and slippers, too."

Just like a collie, I thought. Where the hell is she? It couldn't take her long to put that little thing on.

"She's a wonderful cook, Lloyd. I raised her over a stove . . . "

78

The sales pitch was cut short when Cheryl reentered the room in her new outfit. I clenched my fists and gritted my teeth and then I gritted my fists and clenched my teeth. Mrs. Seltzer was in heaven as she watched me suffer for five minutes with my legs crossed three times around. Cheryl was hanging out all over.

She sat down next to her mother on the bed. "Well, Lloyd, does the color look all right on her?" Mrs. Seltzer adjusted the straps on the swimsuit.

"It looks great. It really does . . ." I sighed, staring intently at Cheryl's voluptuous breasts. "Just wonderful."

"We have to go," declared Mrs. Seltzer abruptly. "Lloyd's got packing to do."

So this was it, I thought, the old Jewish bikini torture.

"Wait!" I cried. "I'll take Cheryl home." Cheryl never looked up. She was playing with my new socks.

"No, Doctor, we don't want to bother you," smiled Mrs. Seltzer triumphantly. "Come on, honey."

"No bother," I remained seated. "It's no bother, really!"

"Bye, Lloyd. Keep in touch, won't you?"

"Yeah, Lloyd, hope you like school." Cheryl bent over to kiss my forehead, and I got a bird's-eye view of the cleavage. That did it. I was paralyzed. I watched helplessly, unable to move, as Cheryl followed her mother out the door.

"It's no bother," I moaned, regaining my power of speech as I heard the car doors slam. I stood up weakly and watched the car pull out of the driveway. "Good-bye, beautiful, bountiful body of Cheryl." I babbled on for about fifteen minutes before wandering into the bathroom to assess my haggard face.

"You fool," I cried at the face in the mirror, "You could have, and you didn't. You *should* have, and you didn't. Suffer—you deserve to suffer."

Suddenly something caught my eye—something that was wrapped neatly and conspicuously around my can of shaving cream. It was fluffy and soft and there was a big number one scrawled across the front. Cheryl's panties! Cheryl's pink panties! She had used the bathroom during her one-act fashion show and, after changing into her bikini, left her panties—for me!

"She wants it!" I shouted jubilantly and ran from the bathroom outside to the front lawn.

"She wants it!" I shouted at the city bus, waving the pink panties. I ran back inside.

"She wants it!" I shouted at the maid who was cleaning out the closet in the hallway.

"I always knew you had a screw loose," she said, shaking her head.

"She'll get it," I resolved as my plane gracefully touched down on the runway of O'Hare International Airport.

13

"Ladies and gentlemen, may I have your attention? Ladies and gentlemen! Thank you. Welcome to your new home. Today you are chemistry and biology majors dedicated to the molecule and the fetal pig. Tomorrow you will be physicians dedicated to the health of mankind."

I was a med student. However, I felt no less frightened than I had as a college freshman. And, just as four years ago academia appeared much more overwhelming than it actually was, an M.D. degree now appeared more unattainable than ever. What if I flunked out? I expected to work hard, but what if I lacked the psychological stability to endure four years of tedious studying? And when it came to working with real patients, would I be able to face the responsibility? Would someone die because of my error? I glanced at the faces of the students around me. What were *they* thinking? At that moment, terrified of the next four years, I felt certain of failure.

Although none of us looked the role, in four years my one hundred and two classmates and I would be M.D.'s. A segment of our class would spend its collective life pulling newborns into the world. Another group would preside over the couch, often deciding whether a patient were sane. Another bunch would find happiness and posterity slicing up the human body. At the moment, we waited in nervous anticipation for the dean of the medical school to continue his orientation speech:

"Your first year of training will unveil to you the secrets of the healthy human body. We will examine how a tasty whipped-cream strawberry cobbler is transformed into energy for a beating heart. We will visualize the miniscule refining systems of the kidney cell under the microscope. We will also see how the human brain is responsible for all your drives, from sex to hunger."

I sat up and started listening more closely.

"The mysteries of disease will be explored in your second year here. We will see why the heart of a healthy Dallas linebacker can, at one moment, be nourishing every muscle and, at the next, collapse into a useless pulp of tissue and vessels. We will learn how the father of French democracy collapsed and died in a matter of seconds because one blood vessel had a 'blow-out.' And, we will learn why the American president who carried this nation out of the depression was confined to a wheelchair."

I was on the edge of my seat, balancing the chair on its two front legs.

"The third and fourth years of your education, ladies and gentlemen, will be spent practicing the science of medicine. We will resuscitate the victim of that heart attack. We will reconstruct that blown-out blood vessel. We will immunize the population against another polio epidemic."

The audience buzzed with enthusiasm as the

professor stepped down. Although we were to confront death in its various guises every day for the rest of our lives, we hoped we would be able to defeat it more often than not. We assumed that our four years of medical school would be an experience of maturation and change. We would become human sponges, absorbing everything necessary to save lives. It was exhilarating to hear a man who "knew" talk with such Hippocratic optimism. At that moment, there was none in that room who wanted to escape even if he could have.

A third figure, a woman, stepped to the speaker's lectern. "Ladies and gentlemen, may I have your attention for a brief bulletin from the administration: This medical institution is plagued by inflation and dwindling federal funds. Regretfully, the burden of this deficit cannot be buffered by our treasury. And so, unfortunately, we have no alternative but to pass this burden on to you, the consumers."

There was an ugly buzzing sound in the audience, and rude hissing and catcalls greeted her final words. I glanced around to see that all prior enthusiasm had suddenly vanished in the face of MORE financial demands. The price of textbooks, lab kits, uniforms and cafeteria food had all gone up—and now tuition, too. The students started chanting "Strike! Strike!" and I joined in for fear of being ostracized if I didn't. Needless to say, we all fully intended to pay the extra bread. We hadn't spent four years of undergraduate shit-shoveling just to be thwarted by the dollar sign.

"You haven't spent four years of undergraduate study just to be stopped by that?" asked my mother over the phone. "Your father and I were notified of the tuition increase weeks ago. Don't you worry about it. You can increase the amount of your loan. Your father and I will be happy to cosign. We know you won't let us down."

"Lloyd, we're proud of you," my father confided, "and this was a big decision you made. You know what I always say . . ."

"If you make a big decision, stick to it no matter what."

"That's right, Lloyd. Now, if you're going to be a doctor, then you're going to have to pay for it. When you *are* a doctor, and making all that money, you'll laugh to think that the cost of your education had ever bothered you."

"All that money?" I echoed.

"Lloyd, Lloyd, don't you worry about it now. My goodness," comforted my mother on the extension, "your education will more than pay for itself."

"But, Mom," I protested, "what if I don't make a lot of money after I get my M.D.?" Somewhere I had come up with the unpopular notion that being a good doctor would be a reward in itself.

"Lloyd, this is a big decision," repeated my father sternly.

"What if I decide to practice medicine in Appalachia?"

Mother chuckled, and Dad cleared his throat.

"What a sense of humor!" said my mother, completely misreading me.

"Mother, I'm serious. What if I struggle through another four years of books and exams and decide to take what I learn to Appalachia or the ghetto?"

"Be serious, Lloyd," cautioned my father. "Your mother and I want only the best for you. We want you nearby. You wouldn't do that to us."

"Do *what* to you?"

"Take all your talent and run off to Appalachia. It would be a hard life, son. Are you sure that's what you want? You're an idealist; you have to learn to be practical."

"Lloyd, we need you here in Washington," added my mother. "Bring all that medical knowledge home to your family and the people who love you."

"We'll see. I gotta go, Mom. Thanks . . . thanks," I stammered. What was I thanking them for? I was confused. "Really, thanks . . . for everything."

14

Anatomy lab is an integral part of medical school. I spent endless hours in a stuffy room with one hundred fellow students and twenty-five corpses, learning what the human body looks like, inside and out. But fewer and fewer med students are getting a taste of this unique experience. Increasingly, plastic human models and television programs are taking the place of actual lab work. Students in many modern institutions are given self-instruction kits that complement the human body in the laboratory.

Gross anatomy lab was an essential initiation for me, but I'm not sure if I was initiated, perverted, or desensitized. My cadaver was a female Caucasian about 45 years of age. The fixation process takes approximately three months. Legal entanglements usually take another six months to a year to resolve (unless the bodies have been willed to science). The cadaver arrives at the lab after a year of being injected and petrified in solutions. The skin is brown, rubbery, and wrinkled. There is a tautness in the texture that makes you shiver whenever you make an incision. The head and pelvic areas have been shaved. If you're lucky, the eyes are closed.

Each corpse was placed on a rusty metal table in front of the small stand that held the lab manual. There were four students per corpse, and we were assigned one, identified by number, on a first-come, first-served basis. Each day when we climbed the four flights of spiraling stairs to the morgue, we raced the other teams, knowing that those who arrived first would get approximately thirty extra minutes of cutting time on their bodies. All the bodies were stored in a large, crowded chest of drawers. Retrieving a cadaver was a team effort; it was cumbersome.

Most people have never spent a good deal of time with a corpse. Many people have never even seen a dead person. And most med students will admit that the first time they saw, touched, and hacked up a corpse, they felt just a bit sick. I felt nauseous, too. Everything I'd ever known about death had come to me in headlines or at funerals. The anatomy lab is not similar. The bodies lying in front of you are NOT people, they are tools. They are no more human than a fetal pig or a dog. You learn to ignore the eyes, the features. You learn to avoid noticing similarities between the corpse and a cousin you once met. You learn to detach yourself from emotion, and from your stomach. And you learn to cut. You learn to tolerate formaldehyde and alcoholic odors. You learn to laugh and joke with your classmates.

Maintaining a sense of humor while hacking up a corpse may sound insensitive. On the contrary, it's absolutely necessary. For most of us, the humor rarely got out of hand. But then there was the type of student every professor feared—the practical joker. Believe it or not, these students viewed a human cadaver as an inexhaustible source of comedy. Our class was "blessed" with four such minds who could be counted on, at least once a month, to disrupt the whole lab, if not the entire university.

The first episode in their continuous series of pranks was the "sex change mystery." One team had been puzzling over a strange set of organs uncovered in their male corpse. The lab manual showed no corresponding organ, and the four students were getting desperate. They finally concurred that the safest bet was cancer so they told the instructor of their finding. The doctor examined the cadaver and then approached the poor souls with his diagnosis.

"Well, gentlemen, it appears that we have some pranksters in our midst. Someone has placed a female organ in the abdomen of your cadaver."

All of us laughed heartily, agreeing that it would be difficult to recognize a uterus in the same body that possessed two testicles. A uterus could, under those circumstances, be mistaken for a tumor.

Their next victim was the poor elderly man who had the misfortune to substitute for the regular janitor of the anatomy building. On his second night, when he was sweeping in the lab, the lights flickered and died. As he groped for the fuse box, four stiffs under white sheets rose from the dissecting table and began to chant. The janitor dropped his broom and dust pan and pulled a pocket-sized Gideon Bible from his trousers.

"Save me, Lord! Save me!"

The four bodies encircled the poor man and began louder incantations. The janitor fumbled through the pages of his Bible and finally came to what he wanted.

"The Lord is my Shepherd. I shall not want. He maketh . . ."

Gradually, the four shrouded figures, their voices subsiding, moved back to the tables and lay down. The janitor kissed his Bible, thanked the Lord, and went back to his sweeping.

Next, the four jokers moved on to the big time—involving the police force in one of their capers. One of them had smashed up a .22 caliber bullet with a hammer and inserted it inside the heart of one of the corpses. Since the elderly female had been thought to have died of old age, there was quite a furor when the bullet was discovered. The FBI was called in, as well as a whole squadron of private detectives hired by the suspicious relatives of the deceased. They would still be trying to solve the "crime" if it weren't for the sharp eye of the city coronor.

"There are no entrance wounds into the body," he said. "This injury would be impossible unless the bullet was fired from *within* the victim." Case closed.

I got my first taste of these guys' special brand of humor on the very first day of anatomy lab—Rip Open the Abdomen Day.

"I can't work on this," I told my lab partner and new roommate from Hawaii, Keone.

"Lloyd, you and Keone go for the liver and the gall bladder," ordered our table captain.

"I can't work on this," I repeated, this time to the table captain.

"What do you mean, Lloyd? This stuff isn't bad at all."

"Her eyes are open! Ethel's eyes are open!" I cried.

My table captain had an older brother who had been to med school so he was expecting the open eyes.

We weren't supposed to know the names of our cadavers, either, but some students had sneaked into the file room. Mine was named Ethel.

Keone came to my rescue by shutting the eyelids.

"What did they feel like?" I whispered.

"Like skin," he replied.

In undergraduate courses, I had messed around with dogs and cats and monkeys. I could stomach anatomy work on *anything*, I had thought. Because of my morbid curiosity, I had actually been looking forward to the day I'd get to hack on a real human corpse.

"Her eyes . . . look!" I whimpered. Ethel's eyes had slowly reopened. Biologically, all that had happened was that the muscles had hardened with the eyes open so that now there was a reflex. But I was sure that Ethel was coming back to life.

Keone shut them again, this time with more force.

The two people at the head of the table were getting impatient, so we started to cut into the abdomen. I was reading the lab manual. It was written like a cookbook, anecdotes and all: "Squeeze the stomach gently with your thumb and forefinger, working your way down the whole length. Did your cadaver pass away with a full tummy?" To me, this was macabre.

"Make a horizontal incision about five inches above the navel," I read. Keone incised beautifully, and our table erupted with gasps of amazement as the abdominal cavity became exposed. There was a guy at our table working on one of the hands, while another one started playing with the liver. I was told to go after the gall bladder.

91

"I can't find it, Keone. It just isn't there."

"Lloyd, it's right here in the book. The gall bladder lies just below the liver at the edge of the rib cage," Keone insisted.

"Damn it, my hand *is* under the liver and the rib cage is scratching the hell out of my wrist. It is *not* here!" I noticed that my rubber surgical glove had been slit by abrasive action against the ribs.

Keone was exasperated. Everything that goes on in gross anatomy lab is timed; everything is a race to get the most done in the least amount of time. The team that first strips its cadaver down to a skeleton usually ends up in the most favorable position, in terms of grades. It takes three months to finish the corpse.

"Lloyd, it's up to us. They have dissected the hand already. They can't work on anything else until we find this damn gall bladder."

"Why not? Why can't they cut up the lungs or the heart or the brain?" I stuck my hand under the rib cage again and started feeling around blindly.

"Because that's not until another day. They can't touch the lungs until we've done steps two and three. The lungs are steps four, five, and six. Now the gall bladder *must* be located in proper order. Dig around down there!"

My table captain and the other kid were visibly shaken by the slowness of the abdominal team. After five minutes of reviewing the lab manual, Keone concluded that something was wrong. He even stuck his own hand under the rib cage to feel the spot where the gall bladder wasn't. "You're right, Lloyd," he said with authority, "somebody ripped it off."

All the other teams were speeding along, making all kinds of noises every time something new was discovered in their corpse. Time was running out; soon the professor would start his routine check of the tables to see who was having trouble—and who would pass.

I was assigned the task of "browsing," i.e., innocently approaching my peers to ask if I could see *their* gall bladders. Meanwhile, my team would work on Ethel, trying to make it look like they were busy with new organs while they waited for the results of my reconnaissance.

It seemed like the class intellectuals always got to do things together. There were the four of them working on a corpse, super-conscientiously. They breathed medicine, wore the same pants for two weeks in a row, and slept with stethoscopes. They were the kind of guys who would write a long thesis and send it to "Marcus Welby, M.D." to be made into a television screenplay. They were the only ones in gross lab that didn't have a name for their cadaver. They knew his real name when he was alive, but they deemed it unprofessional to think of corpses as one would a patient.

"Excuse me," I said politely. Each of the four had his head bowed over the specimen.

"Hey, fellas." I tried the friendly approach.

Still no contact made. I cleared my throat. No luck.

I finally got up the courage to tap one of these diligent dissectors on the shoulder. It was Harry Plum, the Wizard. He stared at me wide-eyed through his horn-rimmed glasses.

"Well?"

"Hey, Harry. How's Ernie coming?"

"Goldman, this cadaver is *not* Ernie. It is cadaver number six. Now what do you want?"

"Oh come on, Harry, why don't you call him Ernie? Everyone else has a name for theirs. After all, he *was* Ernie, right?"

"He *was!* He is now number six. He is now *not* a 'he.' He is now a body—'it.' Number six! Now, what do you want?"

"Harry, I can't find Ethel's—my cadaver's—gall bladder. Any suggestions?"

"Hmmmm." Harry continued to prod and probe Ernie's abdomen. "Interesting. There are many noteworthy considerations for such a biological variant. It is well known, for example, that .25 percent of the world's population is born without a gall bladder. Of course you know that .16 percent develop with an ectopic gall bladder (growing in the wrong place). There is one chance in one thousand that your cadaver is representative of the curiosity *situs inversus*—all the organs are on the opposite side of the body than normally."

"Oh."

"Lloyd, I don't want to mislead you, though. In this country the percentages are slightly lower. It's more like—well, where did your cadaver come from?"

"I dunno."

"There are eleven different theories for this difference . . ."

By number eleven, I could see the professor moving up to our table. I muttered a "thanks anyway" to Harry and sidled up to the next table in line. I should have checked it out first.

94

There were the four class comics, clustered over a body, laughing in low and sinister tones. I approached them with more than slight misgivings about the veracity of any advice they might offer.

"Hey guys. Look, I'm lost. Which way to the gall bladder?" It was a meager and ill-received attempt to share their brand of humor. The four pairs of cunning eyes looked up at me, then slyly at one another.

"Sure, Lloyd," said the biggest smile. "Give me your hand." He guided my sweaty fist through a pile of entrails and placed it right under the liver. All four of them crowded around me. The two who were cutting up the hand even stopped long enough to see if I could find the gall bladder.

"By God! There it is!" I was amazed, but withheld my thank-you. "Hey, it's coming out. It's not even attached!" I withdrew my hand in which a large green avocado was tightly clasped. The foursome erupted into disgusting gales of laughter until the professor looked in our direction.

"Sorry, Lloyd," said one of the four, "but Jeff had that in his lunchbox. We knew someone would be a sucker!" He then guided my hand back into the abdomen where I successfully located the real gall bladder.

I arrived back at Ethel's body just in time for the professor's questions.

"Good morning." He pulled an index card out of his lab gown and read: "Please name and demonstrate the muscles involved in making a fist."

The hand contingent responded without difficulty.

"Fine. Now the muscles used in making a peace sign." The same twosome failed to mention a muscle in the index finger and so they fumbled, trying to duplicate the professor's request with their own hands. When they unintentionally offended our instructor with what appeared to be an obscene gesture, he became impatient and reprimanded them for not being prepared.

"We are not here to waste time," he said acidly. Then, he turned to me. "Okay Goldman, show me the bile duct system originating from the gall bladder."

I began groping around in the same area that the jokers with the avocado had shown me. I *knew* for a fact that what I had found that second time was, indeed, a gall bladder. Yet there was no sign of mine anywhere. The professor just shook his head.

I pulled through the intestines madly trying to locate one of Plum's .16 percent misplaced gall bladders—without luck. The instructor watched me intently, while his breathing became heavier. As a last resort, I abandoned my search and blurted out: "Sir, some .25 percent of the world's population is born without a gall bladder." Eyes shot up from all over the room. Harry Plum glared at me; *he'd* wanted to be the one to impress the professor with that data. The idiots with the avocado started laughing hysterically when they saw me blush.

The professor was not impressed with Plum's data and thoroughly disappointed in Keone and me.

"Goldman. Akana. Look in the right upper abdomen. What is that you see?" Keone and I started comparing the tissue on the surface with that inside the cavity. "What do you see?" repeated the instructor.

"Well, there seems to be a strange mark there on the outside," said Keone timidly.

96

I threw in my two cents. "The tissue on the inside is also . . . strange."

"That, gentlemen, is a scar!"

We looked at each other and nodded.

"And do you know what a scar means?" the professor asked.

"A wound!" I chirped.

"It means that this person had her gall bladder removed before she died. Probably many years before she died." The professor stormed off, scrawling in his grade book.

"Well, shit, Lloyd, it's only the first day. Why should he yell like that?" Keone was as upset as I was.

"I dunno, Keone. Damn it, why didn't we spot that?" I was in misery. "What if that happened to a *live* person?"

Harry Plum's group had finished with Ernie for the day. They put him back in the drawer and Harry came over to our table.

"That was dirty, Lloyd. Real cheap!"

"What else could I do? Besides, what you told me didn't do a damn bit of good."

"I know. I'm sorry," said Harry, patting me on the shoulder. "Listen, I forgot to tell you about a twelfth theory explaining the lower percentage of gall bladder abnormalities in this country as opposed to overseas . . ."

Harry babbled on, but I wasn't listening. I was watching Ethel, whose eyes had reopened during the conversation.

15

The anatomy guest lecturer was finishing his famous presentation on the fifteen muscles it takes to make a smile. With dissecting instruments in one hand and the lab manual in the other, I was sitting restlessly on the edge of my seat awaiting the corny finale:

". . . required that all fifteen muscles synchronize with an exactness of timing . . . it's no wonder that a smile is so hard to come by these days."

Not waiting to chuckle feebly with the rest of the class, I dashed through the swinging doors and up the spiral steps toward the gross lab where we would begin yet another day of carving on the cadaver. We had progressed past the "find and identify the organs" stage and into the "remove and dissect the organs" phase. The competition was still intense, and there was a large throng of students, all clutching lab books and scalpels, following me up the stairs to the morgue.

Triumphantly, I stood first in line while Keone and my other team partners squeezed in behind me to retrieve Ethel from her drawer. The professor arrived.

"Goldman, come here a minute."

I was first in line for the first time in my life, and now he wanted me to lose my place.

"Save my spot," I told Keone.

"Goldman, we've got a problem today," said

99

Dr. Evans gravely. "It's about your cadaver, number eight, I believe."

"That's right, she's number eight."

"Well, the will donating the body to science included a provision, at the request of the family, which may disrupt our lab class today."

I sensed tragedy. They were going to reclaim Ethel!

"Are they going to reclaim our cadaver?" I cried.

"Calm down, Goldman. No, no, they can't take the cadaver, but the family has requested to see the body one more time."

This was shocking. Ethel had been dead quite a while and she looked absolutely *nothing* like she did when she was alive. None of the corpses did. In fact, they all looked the same. There was little if any difference between two white female corpses of the same age bracket.

I went over and told my table mates about the problem. We had to wheel Ethel out into an anteroom and cover her up to her neck with a couple of sheets so the family wouldn't notice that her right arm was gone.

I felt like an amateur mortician as I cleaned our cadaver's face and closed her eyes for the umpteenth time.

"This won't work, Lloyd," complained Keone, "they'll notice that her arm is missing. She looks like a stick."

"Come on, they know she's dead. And they know she's been cut up. They can't expect miracles."

Keone was persistent. "I've got an idea. We'll borrow an arm from Ernie just so it looks right under the sheet." He went over to Harry Plum's table and

100

returned with a badly mutilated left arm.

"That's the wrong one."

"They won't notice. After all, they know she's been dead for eighteen months." Keone dismissed my observation, but I've always believed that if you're going to do something, do it right, even if it's wrong.

"Try to find a right arm," I insisted. "It looks ridiculous."

We couldn't locate an amputated right arm from any of the other corpses so we had to settle for Ernie's. After working on her for about fifteen minutes, we decided our cadaver was as good-looking as she was ever going to be.

"Fine, boys," said the professor. "Now one of you has to stay with the body to make sure they don't try to look at the whole thing." I rushed for the door, but my three classmates beat me to it. I had no choice but to sit down in the corner and don the surgical mask the professor handed me. ("It's better if we look as professional as possible," he explained.) He left the room and in a couple of minutes a woman and two teenaged boys entered the room.

Cadaver number eight, alias Ethel, was completely covered.

I can't believe this is happening, I thought to myself. Nevertheless, I assumed the most solemn air possible. I had no precedent, but I thought solemnity was called for under the circumstances.

"Are you ready to see . . . " I stopped in mid-sentence. What would I call it? The departed? Too funereal. Ethel? That might be too familiar. There was an awkward pause, as I searched my brain for an answer.

101

Finally, in desperation, I blurted, "Ready?"

Somewhat taken aback, the woman replied, "Yes, doctor. Please. This will be the last time for all of us."

The three people approached the table cautiously. I lifted the sheet to expose the head, folding the cover back just below the neck. There was a short gasp from the woman while the two boys stared, their eyes big as saucers.

"Oh my, look at George now!"

George!! My god, I thought, there's been a mistake. How can I tell them this isn't George? I can't, I concluded, glancing at the woman. She's obviously the nervous type—she might faint.

"That's not Dad," said one of the boys. "Dad wasn't bald."

"We have to shave all of the stiff . . . uh . . . the cor . . . all of them," I bungled my way through an explanation.

"Of course it's George," the widow asserted. "I think I know my own husband."

"But he's so skinny," said the younger boy. "His face is so thin and . . . gray."

I could have strangled the kid, but instead I gently explained, "Eth . . . uh . . . he's been gone for a long time."

"Gross," muttered the older son. I jumped, thinking he was referring to gross lab. But he merely yawned and left the room.

That's a relief, I thought. Now if only the other two would leave. The longer they stood there, the more I had to worry about George being Ethel—with Ernie's arm. And the longer they stood there, the faster my team would have to work to catch up with the rest of the class.

"George, George," moaned his wife. "So thin, so gray."

The other son was obviously bored. He headed towards the door, but before leaving turned to me with an accusing look, "That's not Dad. Dad didn't look like that."

Two down, one to go. The widow was still gazing intently at Ethel.

"He looks ... so natural," she observed. "Yes, that's the way he looked when he was asleep. He'd always sleep with his eyes just barely closed and with his right arm draped across his chest like this." She reached for Ernie's arm.

"Wait, Ma'am, don't!" I shouted. Too late. She had found the arm and moved it across Ethel's chest. 1 held my breath. But because she was so wrapped up in her sentimental memories of George, and because the arm was still under the sheet, she didn't notice that it wasn't connected.

A gasp of relief escaped me just as Harry Plum burst into the room. Rudely ignoring the woman, he sputtered angrily, "Lloyd, I need that arm back. We're on step number twelve and we need the arm . . ."

"Out, get out of here!" I hissed, and Harry scurried out the door—like a rat.

"Well," sighed the widow, "he lived a good life . . ."

"Yes ma'am," I agreed.

"Young man," she said turning to me, "you don't know what this visit has done for me—I feel years younger."

That's funny, I thought. I've aged considerably.

She left the room, wiping the tears from her eyes. I covered up Ethel respectfully and wheeled her back into the lab room, dropping off Ernie's arm on the way to my station.

16

The more I thought about Ethel's family reunion, the more it got to me. I mean, if death isn't sacred, what is? As soon as classes were finished for the day, I hurried home to the room I shared with Keone in the old Windsor Hotel. To ease my depression, I unwound in a tub of hot water while reading over my most recent pile of letters from the home front. Grandmother Schlessel was working diligently, trying to fix me up with one of the cross-country entries in her ledger book of prospective brides. The girls would rarely turn out to be my type, but, for Grandmother's sake, I would always give them a call.

My grandmother's letters were of particular interest to me, for they invariably contained "hints for health and long life":

Dear Lloyd,

I have read your letter to your mother, how beautiful you write. I know you are smart and have a good feeling for others. You're giving good advice. I think you will go far in your profession. Only stay well. I should live to see you in your gown and cap and getting your diploma. Now, dear grandson, as far as your diet is concerned, don't eat bread, chicken, or meat. Eat Jell-o every day. I gave corn flakes to the birds. They wouldn't eat it so I don't eat it. Send away to the Jell-o people for a recipe book. Take a couple of milk of magnesia pills about once a week. It coats the stomach and helps the digestion. Eat cooked vegetables. Put a glass of table salt in your bath. Take one enema once a month to clean your lower bowels. Don't eat too much at one meal. You should better eat five small meals than three heavy meals. Put your feet up when you study. Make sure you sleep seven or eight hours a day. Don't eat ice, no ice cream. Hungry? Eat a baked apple with a little cream on top. Chew on a few raisins for when you are hungry, that will not make you fat. Use a cream to wash your face and that will keep you beautiful. Get a one-a-day vitamin or B-12 and don't love too much, you know what I mean. If you observe all this you will live to be 100 years of age. The reason I tell you this is because I love you.

Love,
Grandmother

The Seltzer household also corresponded quite heavily, but Cheryl's mother usually contributed the bulk of the conversation. Cheryl would write a few lines in Jack 'n Jill style, discussing the weather or recent developments in her favorite soap operas, "The Doctors" and "General Hospital." She would sign all her letters, "From, Cheryl." Mrs. Seltzer would follow with a three-page postscript that always began: "I just wanted to say hello . . . " She would tell of Cheryl's growing interest in medicine and of her fascinating new hobby, keeping a scrapbook about medicine from all *Time, Reader's Digest* and *Newsweek* magazines. She would proudly boast that Cheryl was finally learning to understand "Marcus Welby, M.D." The most cheerful news from Mrs. Seltzer was that Cheryl had opened a special bank account to save money for a visit to Chicago. Since presently she had $8.35 in the account, I realized that her visit would be years away; however, I was more than willing to wait.

In the meantime, I thought to myself, I would date as many girls as humanly possible. Why shouldn't I cash in on the prestige afforded the medical profession? I mean, what girl *wouldn't* date a med student?

My first problem was communicating the fact that I, Lloyd Goldman, was a med student. Initially, I chose the direct approach. Daily, I would stroll through the "other side" of the campus, where the female population outnumbered the male. If a chick happened to turn me on, I'd saunter up to her and casually remark, "Hi! I'm Lloyd Goldman and I'm a med student."

Logical, right? Cut the small talk and get right to the point. However, for some reason, my technique invariably induced an undesirable response.

"The uniform, Goldman, the uniform," counseled Keone upon hearing of my troubles.

But of course—the classic whites!

Next day, clothed in snow-white from head to toe, I made my usual tour of the campus. This time two coeds actually spoke to me.

"Hey, I know you," said the first. "You work in the cafeteria at Pierce Hall."

"How about an extra portion of dessert tonight, babe?" wheedled the second.

It was some time until I learned that the key to success was the black bag. Oh sure, a stethoscope hanging from a pocket and a clearly labeled medical text under the arm can't hurt—just for insurance. But carry a black bag and girls approach *you*. (Of course, I never bothered to notice the girls who were turned off by my pretentiousness.)

In reality, my black bag turned out to be more of a Pandora's box than the solution to my sexual frustrations. At first, I spent quite a bit of time pursuing girls—many of whom had an ulterior motive in allowing themselves to be seduced by a medical student. After all, medical advice is expensive, and my guess is that these girls thought they could repay me without cutting into their budgets.

Most of the girls I dated wanted help with medical problems ranging from venereal disease to irregularity. Even the ones who were in relatively sound physical condition would always come up with some turn-off in the middle of a romantic scene. There were so few of these scenes in my life that I wanted each one to be precious and perfect.

For example, once I was snuggled up with a girl on the second-hand sofa in my hotel room. The light bulb had just burned out and my transistor radio was playing softly—the static barely noticeable. As I drew her close to me, a tender voice whispered, "Lloyd, do birth control pills *really* cause blood clots?"

108

Picture this scene—the back seat of my Pontiac, the city park, the full moon, the windshield fogged by two panting lovers. As I casually unzipped her, she remarked, "Lloyd, I'm two weeks late."

Then, there was the canoe ride—another girl, the brisk nighttime air, the warm quilt blanket. "Oh, Lloyd," she breathed, "please check the other one, too."

Even if I wasn't really a doctor, I was already a victim of the hypochondriacs' syndrome. These girls thought, in all sincerity, that knowing a doctor personally not only entitled one to free medical advice, but also increased the chances of improved health and longer life expectancy.

I had never, in all my years of dreaming about the medical profession, seen the obvious disadvantages of being a doctor. Professionally, an M.D. is regarded as a highly respectable member of the community. Personally, a doctor is viewed somewhat mystically by relatives, suspiciously by colleagues, and deliciously by opportunists.

17

"Are you sure that's the breast? It looks like fat."

"Let's see if you can tell the difference between the heart and the bladder."

"I always get the mouth mixed up with the vagina."

If gross anatomy creates problems, microscopic anatomy is far worse. Here, the medical student is allowed to zone in on the human body at the cellular level. An innocent eavesdropper would be shocked to hear such ignorance coming from the mouths of would-be physicians, but everything is confusing when viewed under the microscope. Very few ninth-grade biology students would have any trouble telling the difference between the heart and the bladder on a dissecting table, yet the muscle cells that pump blood so majestically out of the heart to every corner of the body are the same type that send your urine rushing madly out of the bladder after a 16-ounce ginger ale. The cells that add that sensual curve to a 36-24-36 bathing beauty are the same ones that add the paunch to the belly of a middle-aged man. No one over age ten would have any trouble distinguishing between a mouth and a female vagina (what other kind is there?), yet the cells which line the female reproductive assembly are the same kind that coat the oral cavity. Peering through a microscope, a freshman med student often gets confused. As long as this confusion doesn't carry over into his private life, he'll survive.

Even after I had chopped through the human body and eye-balled it under the microscope, I was only half-made. Phase two is learning how the machinery works. The physiology lab fills this gap. This place is a zoological carnival; I was surrounded by live dogs, cats, goats, frogs, and monkeys. I learned that wiring a cat and shocking its brain in the hunger center will cause it to smack its lips. Altering a dog's circulation will cause its pulse to jump dangerously. Dropping a certain solution in a rabbit's eye will enlarge the pupil, making the insides of the eyeball more clearly visible. Despite the fact that the university took every precaution against the possibility of our inflicting pain on the animals (the living specimens were asleep throughout the experiments), it took quite an emotional adjustment, on my part, to participate in physiology lab. For the first time, I began to realize the full implications of what it would mean to work on living creatures. Now I was cutting on an animal; in a few years, I would be cutting on a living person.

Meanwhile, I counted myself among the animals. Medical students become their own guinea pigs. A typical weekly homework assignment during freshman year was to run around the block ten times, hooked to a special heart monitor, and give a pint of blood. For the sake of science, medical students are explored from every anatomical orifice. For ten dollars, volunteers would consent to anything from swallowing a stomach tube to submitting to a rectal exam. The routine varied from week to week, but I was usually exhausted, humiliated, and disgusted by Friday evening.

My assignments were relatively innocuous compared to a class demonstration that shook up the students, the professors, and the administration as well. We were studying the effects of a commonly used drug on various nerves in the body. The professor asked for a volunteer to take the drug and then allow his bodily systems to be monitored. Always seeking an opportunity to perform before a live audience, the four jokesters fell all over each other volunteering. Finally, one was selected.

Before submitting to such an experiment, the volunteer must fill out a permission slip to absolve the school of any legal entanglements. One of the questions asked is: "What financial value do you place on your life at the present time?" The joker drew quite a laugh from everyone, including the professor, when he arrived at the modest sum of $5,000,000. After a few more minutes of clowning, he took the drug, and we all crowded around to chart the expected changes in his parasympathetic nervous system.

Things were going smoothly until suddenly his heart stopped beating. We were all stunned. We couldn't believe what our eyes told us and looked to the professor for reassurance, only to find him rushing to the emergency medical equipment that was always kept close by. Just as he began to pound on the jokester's chest, the heart began to pump again.

It was some time before the class recovered from the shock of what had happened. Although the jokester regained consciousness and suffered no ill effects from the few seconds his heart had stopped, every last one of us was overwhelmed by the thought of what *might* have happened. Even the jokester was frightened and was remarkably subdued for days afterward. We had been made to realize, in the harshest way possible, that we must always be prepared for the unexpected. No matter how many times a doctor has administered a drug or performed an operation, something can go wrong. The most harmless medical procedure may have serious consequences.

The twenty-four hour urine specimen was perhaps the most embarrassing project. At least, that's how it was for me. Each class member was responsible for collecting his urine for twenty-four hours.

In my case, the urine assignment coincided most inconveniently with a dinner engagement at the home of one of my professors, the chairman of the Anatomy Department, Dr. Robert Evans. He lived in a white-pillared mansion in the suburbs, the same as all the other department chairmen at the university. I didn't have many clothes so I arrived bundled in my father's World War II jacket, carrying a paper bag in each hand. In my right hand was a jug full of urine, in my left was a bottle of sparkling burgundy wine.

I rang the bell. An aristocratic, gray-haired lady appeared at the door, smiling.

"Mr. Goldman, I'll bet."

"Yes, ma'am."

Right hand urine, left hand burgundy wine.

"I always look forward to these evenings with Bob's—the Professor's—students. May I take your coat?"

Right hand urine, left hand wine.

114

"Thank you, ma'am."

I carefully put each bag down on the table in the hallway—to the right, the urine; to the left, the burgundy wine.

I took off my jacket, and she hung it up.

"Dr. Evans is in his study. Shall we wait in the living room?" She motioned down the hall.

"Yes, ma'am, but first—a token of my appreciation for your hospitality." I exhaled an ill-founded sigh of relief as I handed the gentle woman the bag on the right.

"How thoughtful!" She stepped into the dining room and placed the bag on the mantle over the fireplace. Then we adjourned to the living room where two little girls were awaiting my arrival. They were introduced as Heather and Christine. They acted very dignified for seven- and nine-year-olds. Heather, at seven, was a brunette whose hair was swept up into one of those elaborate coiffures that make little girls look twenty-five and ready to be shawled in mink. Christine was a Mary Poppins character, a distinguished little blond with a British accent that she must have learned by listening to Paul McCartney.

Munching on caviar and crackers, we bullshitted about a new genus of bee that makes grape-flavored honey, and about noteworthy events like the latest birdwatcher's convention. I had studied up ahead of time so I wouldn't be at a loss for conversation.

At last, Dr. Evans arrived. He was tall and predictably gray-haired (professors start dyeing their hair that color around age thirty), with matching sideburns and a neatly groomed goatee that made him look like Prince Albert on the tobacco pouch. He was the perfect figure to head this family—they could have posed for a portrait on a carry-out box of Colonel Sanders' chicken.

"Good to see you, Mr. Goldman," he greeted me.

"Shall we sit down to dinner?" asked Lady Evans.

Dinner was served in an enormous dining room on a long, narrow mahogany table. After depositing damask napkins on their laps, my hosts bowed their heads in prayer.

Christine: "Lord, make us truly grateful . . . "

The urge to go came over me.

Heather: "God is great, God is good . . . "

I knew it would happen as soon as we sat down. I squirmed about in my seat, attempting to find a more comfortable position for my bladder.

Lady Evans: "Bless us, O Lord, in these Thy gifts . . ."

I began to pray silently—for five minutes of comfort. I just can't get up now. I just can't get up now. I just . . .

Dr. Evans: "Father, we bow our heads to give Thee thanks . . ."

I clenched my hands, gritted my teeth, and prayed out loud: "Dear God, give us strength to overcome our weaknesses . . . excuse me."

I jumped out of my chair and made a desperate dash to the brown paper bag on the hallway table. The Evans family was still bowed in prayer and I wondered if they knew I was through with my invocation.

I stumbled down an adjoining hallway, opening strange doors—a closet, a pantry, a cloak room, a laundry room—but *no bathroom!* With no other alter-

116

native, I slipped into the cloak room. Smothered by jackets and minks, I ripped open the bag and found—a full bottle of sparkling burgundy wine!

This was truly the most frightening experience of my entire first year of medical training. With my bladder distended to the maximum two quart capacity, I couldn't even express a grunt of discomfort for fear of losing a few precious drops of my twenty-four hour urine collection. My body was one big spasm as I walked cautiously back to the dining room table, carefully avoiding any unnecessary bodily jerks.

My apologetic smile was met by four curious expressions. The professor politely avoided the subject of my departure and began talking when I resumed my chair.

"Mr. Goldman, throughout the year I invite a few of the medical students over to my house. This gives me an opportunity to get some fresh, constructive criticism of the anatomy course. In this way I've been able, so far, to adjust the curriculum to the needs of each new class of students. Please let loose. Relax . . . pour out your problems."

I clutched the arms of my chair, not daring to even look at the bowl of simmering soup in front of me. Out of the corner of my eye I spotted my salvation on the ledge of the fireplace—my gift to this prestigious family, a jug half-filled with my own urine. The professor continued:

"Speak up, Goldman. Don't be shy."

"Sir, I . . . "

Lady Evans interrupted with an attempt to make me relax, something I really didn't want to do.

"Son, many students are scared of Bob because of his position and the fact that he is a well-known author and researcher—but don't let that stop you. Take my word for it, and I've lived with him for twenty-five years, he may not look it but he is a youngster at heart. Talk to him like you would talk to one of your peers."

"Lady, if I relax at this moment . . . "

Christine added her fake-English two cents: "Don't be afraid of Father—he's a real human being, too."

Brilliant! I wished the kid would stop slurping her soup.

Little top-heavy Heather spoke out from beneath her bird's nest in a voice that makes all seven-year-olds sound cute, accompanied by a seven-year-old's obnoxious smile that appeals to everyone:

"Daddy loves everybody."

The whole family laughed out loud as I strenuously balanced my bladder. I could feel the muscles giving way. In a last attempt to save face, and keep dry, I blurted out, " 'Scuse me, folks, but where's the restroom?" I thought "restroom" was more refined than "john," or even "bathroom."

"Use the one at the head of the stairs," said the lady of the house, none too quickly.

Without further explanation, I jumped up, raced to the fireplace, grabbed the brown bag, and flew upstairs.

For the next four minutes and twenty-three seconds I was in heaven. I didn't want to leave, even after I was finished. It was so nice up there, just me and my jug and all the privacy we needed. It had been a relief, to say the least, when the dike had given way.

Hesitant . . . embarrassed . . . and frightened, I re-

118

turned to my hosts. Dr. Evans addressed me somewhat suspiciously.

"Say, Goldman, wasn't that a bottle of wine you carted off to the john with you?"

"Sir," I replied firmly, "today the freshman medical class was assigned a task that calls for twenty-four hours of seclusion."

Christine and Heather giggled at my serious tone.

"I did not observe that seclusion and now I've suffered the consequences."

A moment of silence.

Suddenly, Dr. Evans broke into laughter. "Why Lloyd, I'll never forget my first year of medical school when I had to get that twenty-four hour specimen and I had an important date with Mildred, here . . . "

"Robert!" clucked Mrs. Evans sternly.

"Anyway," chuckled the professor, "I'm glad we didn't decide to pour some of your 'wine' before dinner . . . "

"Not as glad as I am," I replied as I reached for my soup spoon.

18

I was broke and I needed a job. But it couldn't be just *any* job. It had to be a job that didn't cut into my studies or my sleep. Keone had a suggestion.

"How about a sperm bank?"

"What?" I grabbed a leaflet from his hand and read about a clinic nearby that needed donors, at fifteen dollars a shot, for a sperm bank. Sperm banks were catching on because of highly sophisticated techniques that allowed for freezing, transporting, thawing, and artificially depositing the sperm in the womb of a woman who wished to have a child. The women were almost always married to infertile husbands.

I called the clinic, and they told me they welcomed my services.

Midnight, the next night. The phone was ringing in the room, and Keone was cursing in Hawaiian.

"Hello," I grumbled, preparing a verbal attack on the late caller.

"Mr. Goldman, this is the Harding Clinic. We'd like you to drop a vial of your sperm by the night depository window at the East Gate."

"Now?! Why do you want it at this hour?"

The man explained to me that my sperm were needed for a woman who wanted a baby with some of my characteristics. She had phoned Harding earlier in the evening requesting that the "juice" be sent to her as soon as possible, since she was ovulating at that time of the month. I hung up, not caring why she had chosen my features, just wondering how in God's name I was supposed to summon the strength that late at night.

I managed, with God's help, and I left the sperm at the clinic. Two days later, the same man called again with the same request. This time there was a girl in my room. After I had hung up, I sat down on the bed where she was lying.

"Lloyd, what's the matter?" She started stroking my hair.

"Nothing. I guess we'll have to cut the evening short. I've gotta—go to work." I looked at her for approval.

"Okay, but first come here."

"No, I can't." I shook my head vigorously.

"Why? Why not?" She was obviously hurt by my refusal to cooperate in the seduction.

"Because . . . I . . . er . . . have to save myself." I knew this line wouldn't go over too well and I was right.

"Don't give me that line," she squawked. "You've got another girl." She hopped out of bed and started straightening her clothes.

"No, no. Believe me," I grabbed her hand and started petting it gently, "I really *do* have to save my . . . energy for work."

"You drag me over here, undress me, and practically . . . "

"Please, I'll make it up to you."

It was no use. My lady friend hustled herself out of my room.

Somehow I managed to comply with the request of my "employers." By now I was thirty dollars richer but minus one girl friend and about six ounces of vital bodily fluids. I hadn't counted on the demand for my sperm being so great.

Three days later the phone rang again. "The sperm count was low on that last vial," complained the voice. "What did you do, dilute it?"

"Don't blame me," I shouted back, "you can't expect high-test when you come back for a fill-up every other day!"

I hung up the phone and pondered my dilemma. Three times a week, by myself—this was too much. Fifteen dollars or no fifteen dollars, my new job was unhealthy for me. I picked up the phone later that afternoon when the man from Harding called to pester me some more.

"*Where is your sperm?!*" clamored the raspy voice.

"I've still got it at the factory. Listen, I've decided to quit. This is a lousy set-up. I'm not equipped with the stamina or the ego to play long-distance baby-maker any more."

"Can't take doing it yourself, huh?" chuckled the voice.

"Don't be crude! It just gets a little tiring and, if you'll pardon the pun, it takes a lot out of me. My sex life is shot to hell. Instead of girls, I'm having affairs with test tubes and sterile vials."

"All right. We can't stop you if you want to quit. Only, please, just fill this one last order."

"Oh . . . ok," I grumbled.

A few minutes later, full vial in hand, I hopped

into my car and turned the ignition key. Nothing happened.

No! It can't break down now. I refuse to do a refill on this order.

I sat there for another five minutes desperately trying to start my car. Finally, I gave up, jumped out of the car, and ran back to my room. I leafed wildly through the phonebook until I came to the page marked "taxis." I called the first company on the page.

"This is an emergency," I yelled at the woman who answered the phone. "Send a cab to the Windsor Hotel right away. There's a vial of emergency medicine that must go out to Harding Clinic immediately."

I returned to the entrance of my building. Within minutes a cab pulled up, brakes screeching.

"Someone call a cab to go to Harding with some medicine?" asked the driver.

"Me," I answered. "Here it is." I handed him the vial labeled "Sperm bank from L. Goldman." "Guard this vial with your life, and hurry."

The cab driver sped away and I returned to my room, whistling happily. A half-hour later the phone rang.

"What's the big idea, Goldman?" asked the same clinic voice who had called earlier.

"My car broke down," I explained. "I didn't want to have to go through *that* again."

"Very funny, wise guy. We haven't had that much excitement in years. Your cab driver pulled up with a police escort. The cop wanted to book him when he found out what was in the vial. If I were you I wouldn't call any more cabs for a while."

124

"I'll keep that in mind, sir. You can take me off your payroll now." And with that I hung up on my last call from the Harding Clinic.

A month or so later when I got my final check for the last sperm deposit, a note from one of the technicians at the clinic was enclosed:

Dear Mr. Goldman,

You'll be happy to know that the recipient of your sperm, whose name cannot be revealed to you, finally became pregnant from the injections she had received over a four-day period last month. I am sure you will be pleased to know that you have given the gift of life to a new human being, and the gift of motherhood to a wonderful woman.

I have to admit that, at the time, I did feel quite good about the pain and exhaustion I had endured for this poor childless woman. I even pinned the little note to the bulletin board and gloated openly in front of Keone.

My joy lasted about nine months, until one day Keone burst into the room and threw a copy of the evening paper on my bed. On Page 5C or somewhere in the back there was an item entitled "Woman Sues Sperm Bank":

A Los Angeles woman filed a million dollar law suit against the Harding Institute of Chicago today for allegedly falsely representing to her the treatment she would be receiving in the administration of artificial insemination . . . .

125

The woman was complaining because the child she had delivered was dark and small-boned with curly hair and brown eyes. The suit alleged that the woman had requested the sperm of a man with a genetic history of mezomorphy—medium height, well-built. Also, claimed the news article, she had specifically requested a father donor with blond hair and blue eyes.

Keone stood before me, laughing triumphantly in his high little voice and scoffing at my anonymous role in this legal crisis.

"You can't prove it was *my* sperm," I cried, almost certain that it *was* my sperm.

"Face the facts, Lloyd," jeered Keone. "Those *are* your characteristics, and it *has* been nine months."

Keone was right.

A million dollars is a lot of money, I thought. I knew people who would pay that much just to *have* a Jewish son. This lady was going to court because her child looked like *me!* The forty-five dollars I'd earned during that one week nine months ago would never compensate for the humiliation my roommate was going to make me endure because of the episode of the cross-country sperm.

19

At the beginning of my sophomore year, Keone and I moved into a large old house with six other medical students. The rent was minimal and the conditions were decadent. The house had not been lived in, legally, for two years, yet there were numerous calling cards left by vagrants, tramps, and psychotics who had camped there at one time or another.

Our first order of business was the tree growing in the living room. We had to chop it down and repair the floor. That process took about two weeks and in that time we encountered numerous snakes, opossums, roaches, and foot-long rats—all of which came in handy for impromptu dissection sessions in the kitchen laboratory we had rigged up.

Since there were eight of us and only five bedrooms, a few of us had to take turns sleeping in beds. It seemed to me that I ended up sleeping in a makeshift bed squeezed into a clothes closet or the bathroom a disproportionate amount of the time. Since Keone was paying a larger portion of the rent, he got his choice of rooms and decided on the living room, the largest and most well-preserved area in the house. He barricaded himself behind odds and ends of lumber for a full week while he refurbished his quarters. When he was through, the place looked like a sheik's bower. There was silk everywhere and wall-to-wall shag carpeting. The walls had been repainted and there was a chandelier in the center of the room over the eight-foot oval bed. Upon seeing this arrangement, all of us became hostile toward Keone.

"What the hell is this?" I growled at him as he lay on his bed eating olives.

"This is my room. I need comfort and I want to feel at home."

Keone came from a very wealthy family on the island of Kauai, so I assumed this was the standard of living to which he was accustomed.

"Yeah, but Keone . . . look around you. The rest of us are living in a sty. Good God, your room looks like a Manhattan brothel."

"You fellows are welcome to do whatever you wish with your own rooms. Just remember who pays the rent." His eyes narrowed as he pronounced these last words.

"Big deal," I said. "You pay ten dollars more per month than the rest of us. You're living in the Hilton, and I'm sleeping in the john." I ranted on, but Keone ignored me. He had turned on his new television set.

Since the house was fairly large, a few of the more industrious residents, myself included, decided to use some of the extra space for independent medical research. I had long since given up my dreams of finding an answer to cancer but I thought that a little homework might prove fruitful in other areas—for instance, high blood pressure.

We all started "borrowing" things from the labs at school. I brought home a human brain while two of the other guys smuggled a heart, a kidney, and a small intestine into the house. Within a week, we had collected enough parts to reconstruct an entire human body. We managed to steal a few pints of formaldehyde to preserve the organs, but the odors in the house became stronger and stronger. Keone, who had not participated in the heists, was outraged.

"*My* room smells! The whole house smells. You've got brains in the kitchen, a heart in the icebox and, worst of all, I sit down on the toilet and there's a bucket full of intestines under the sink. I don't come home from school so I can sleep in a gross anatomy lab. I pay the rent around here and I want this stuff gone by tomorrow."

He harangued us for about an hour until one of the other guys threatened to dump the bucket of intestines over his head. Then he went back into his room and sulked. I approached him later that night to explain to him some of my new theories on leukemia, but Keone would have no part of it.

"You're a spoiled pig," I said angrily. "We don't bring buckets of guts home just to bother you. We're trying to learn something."

"Come on, Lloyd," he said sarcastically, "don't tell me you're actually *serious* about all this. You get to see plenty of brains and hearts at school. You fellows just do this to bother me."

Keone had been paranoid all his life, so his attitude didn't surprise me. I knew he would never believe that my intentions were good, even after I apologized for the sickening odors.

That night Keone came running into the bathroom

to wake me. "Lloyd! Lloyd! Make them stop!" He was frantic and sweaty and near delirium. "Make them leave me alone."

I wasn't really close to any of the other guys living in the house but I knew them well enough to know they wouldn't molest a paranoid. I made a quick bed check and found all of them sound asleep.

"They're all asleep," I reported to Keone, who was still mumbling incoherently. He grabbed my hand and led me into his bedroom-living room where he sat me down on the bed and, with a finger to his lips, motioned for silence.

"Listen, listen!" he whispered as he clutched my arm.

I heard a strange scratching noise coming from the other side of the wall. I ran into the adjoining bedroom, but the occupants were all asleep.

"There's nothing there," I assured Keone.

"I still hear it," he whimpered, trembling.

Sure enough, the noise was louder. It sounded like someone rubbing a handful of corn flakes on sandpaper. I put my ear up against the wall and concluded that the noises were being made by a living creature. I ran and got a small hammer out of the icebox and started banging loudly on the wall. The din increased, especially when everyone else woke up and started swearing loudly. Diplomatically, I went from room to room explaining the mystery. Everyone except Keone went back to sleep.

I hurried back to Keone's room and started ripping the wallpaper off a lower corner of the east wall. Keone panicked.

130

"Damn you—you're ruining my room . . . "

"You want me to stop this noise, don't you?"

He covered his eyes as I pounded the plaster wall until I had fashioned a hole about two feet in diameter. I rushed back into the bathroom where I got Spiro, Harvey Durham's cat. Spiro, who was named for the bacteria, was reportedly able to devour a Volkswagen if he was hungry enough. He was twenty-four pounds of hair and claws and teeth. I was confident that Spiro could kill just about anything in the world, so I stuck him down the hole in the wall.

The noises stopped instantly . . . completely. No screaming, no hissing, no growling. Finally, Spiro emerged from the hole, proudly carrying one of those foot-long rats that I'd seen, only dead, when we moved in. The rat that he was carrying was also dead—now. Spiro deposited it on the luxurious carpet in Keone's room. Evidently Spiro was not hungry, but nonetheless he realized that his duty was to dispatch the rodent to rat heaven. I was very proud of him, but Keone was not.

"Rat blood on my rug!" he hissed, grabbing a tribal hunting spear from its place of honor on the wall. Spiro fled and I fled, leaving Keone to do whatever he wanted with the dead rat.

20

As my sophomore medical year dragged into the winter quarter, Keone's paranoia became contagious. The whole class was manifesting symptoms that appeared concomitantly with whatever disease was described in that day's lecture.

After the lecture on heart disease, we rushed to the clinic every time we had heartburn or indigestion. Cholesterol levels were posted in the kitchen, and for an unknown reason Keone started washing the salt off his pretzels. He even gave up olives. A couple of other guys started on an all-fish diet and got dysentery. "Our hearts are healthy," they staunchly asserted as they wretched on the floor. I tried running track to keep my heart strong until I read about a guy in Miami who collapsed and died of a heart attack while jogging.

The day after the dermatologist spoke to us about skin cancer, we all carried umbrellas to school to protect our fair skin from killer ultra-violet rays. Keone covered himself with a dark coat, a face mask, Coppertone on the exposed areas around his eyes, and leather gloves to protect his hands. He developed a rash from the humidity.

The day after the lecture on lung cancer, the smokers in the class gave up cigarettes for cigars. The next day we had a discussion on cancer of the lip, and all the cigar smokers gave up their cigars for much milder pipes. Then, the next day was the big lecture on tongue cancer, so the pipe smokers lapsed into hysterical nicotine fits; they didn't dare put anything in their mouths. Non-smokers claimed that they had been stricken with tuberculosis the day after the lung lecture.

The most dismal of all was the morose lecture on venereal disease. True to form, all of us who were not married (and a few who were) became fanatical celibates, taking an oath that would assure us of clean bodies—if decidedly unhealthy minds. This lull in the social life lasted about two weeks. Then, upon hearing a lecture on mental disorders caused by anxiety and repression, our half-crazed class decided that sex was indeed healthy and necessary, as long as we were somewhat selective about partners and meticulous about hygiene.

Unlike the rest of us, Keone's paranoia did not subside with the passing of time. When the rest of us went back to cigarettes, Keone remained rigid. He still washed his pretzels and refused olives. He massaged his heart every night before he went to bed in case it should stop as soon as he shut his eyes, thus giving his rescuers a head start on reviving him. It seemed like Keone got a new vaccination every day—smallpox, tetanus, beriberi, anything he could find in a medical journal. He was the only person I have ever met who got booster shots, for *everything,* every month. Still, he couldn't escape the hand of fate.

One day, after his routine self-examination, he came to me with tears in his eyes.

"Lloyd, I'm packing up. Going back to Hawaii."

"What's the matter, Keone? We've made it through the first year; we don't have exams for another month; and you're doing great in school."

"It's not the work. I've got cancer of the colon." He said it with such certainty I thought he must have found something. We had had, that very day, a lecture on cancer of the colon.

"You've got *what?*"

"Here, come here." Keone lay down on the bed. "Now if I get into just the right position . . . I was on my left side with my left leg extended . . . " He twisted around and, with his hand, finally found what he was looking for. "Aha! Now feel this mass. Cancer of the colon. I'm sure of it."

I could feel a mass the size of a golf ball in his abdomen. I was stunned. Maybe Keone was really sick—maybe it *was* cancer! The lump was on his left side, about three inches from the navel.

"It's nothing," I reassured him, "probably nothing at all."

I had serious doubts. One of the case histories reported in the lecture had been of a 28-year-old man whose cancer of the colon had been detected by a doctor who had merely palpated the young man's abdomen and found the mass. Keone and I had both been to that lecture and heard the results: three months of X-ray therapy, a six-month course with toxic drug administration, seven months later metastasis to the brain, and a grotesque downhill progression accompanied by many nausea-producing symptoms.

"I'm going home, Lloyd. It will be wine and women for my last nine months. I've got to have some fun before my brain is hit."

I began to regret all the mean things I'd done to Keone even though everything I did to Keone was done in friendship but mistaken for enmity. The poor fellow had spent the last year of his life dissecting bodies and cramming for anatomy exams. What a way to go.

I thought that there was a good possibility of saving him by removing the colon before the cancer spread. Better a colostomy than destruction of the brain.

"Why don't you go to the infirmary," I advised. "You know—just in case."

The purpose of going to the infirmary was getting someone there to refer you to the nationally famous university clinic. You need a referral before you can be treated at the clinic. I was sure they would refer Keone to a gastroenterologist—a tummy man.

"They aren't open now," complained Keone, starting to cry again.

"What kind of an infirmary is it if it's open all the time? Look Keone, let's go to bed. Tomorrow the mass may disappear. Who knows? I'll wake you up at 7 a.m. so you can rush right over there if you're still worried."

He slowly peeled off his clothes, put on some faded black pajamas, crawled into bed, and turned off the light without another word. I sensed that he was blaming me for his cancer.

I waited until he was asleep and crept out into the night. I ran as fast as I could to the medical library and spent five hours reading every article published since 1945 on cancer of the intestine. When I staggered back into the house at 6 a.m., Keone was staring at the ceiling—either wide awake or stone dead.

"You okay?" I whispered.

"As well as can be expected for a man with nine months to live," Keone replied bitterly. "Where have you been? Out celebrating my death?"

"You aren't going to die. Damn you, I've been at the library reading about your cancer of the colon."

Keone sat up. "I'm sorry. You really spent the whole night there just for me?" He couldn't believe that anyone would spend the whole night in the library for *anything*.

"I read everything," I boasted, "but there are so many variations of this type of cancer—I mean the case histories were so different, you know. I just couldn't pin anything down." I was so tired I could hardly talk.

"What do you think? Do you think I'm going to live?"

"We don't even know if you've got anything yet," I reminded him. "Don't look so disappointed. I know you've been searching for an ailment for six months now, but don't get your hopes up."

With that, Keone collapsed back onto the bed. He stared at the wall for another hour before leaving for the clinic.

When he returned, some three hours later, I was fast asleep. Keone decided that I didn't deserve to sleep while he was dying. "Wake up, Lloyd. Wake up."

I opened one eye. "Did you see the doctor?"

"Yes. He referred me to the university clinic, the gastroenterologist."

"Yeah? Whadesay?"

"More tests."

I opened both eyes. I'd never be able to go to sleep

137

now. I told Keone I'd go to the clinic with him later in the day to get his results. In the meantime, I tried to cheer him up, but he wouldn't laugh at my jokes. We left at noon for the clinic.

I waited for three hours while Keone underwent a grueling series of examinations.

"We have completed our most extensive set of tests on you, Keone," said the tummy man.

Keone didn't say a word. He just gritted his teeth stoically.

"It *could* be cancer," said the doctor, "but then again, it could be something else. Lie down here." The doctor felt around the mass and started squeezing it, a procedure I considered dangerous.

"What are you doing?" I asked.

The tummy man looked at me with contempt. "Just sit still, young man. I think I'm getting to the root of this problem."

Keone was breathing heavily and grinding his teeth. Suddenly, he gave a short gasp. "What did you do to me?" he screamed at the doctor.

"I have cured your cancer," laughed the gastro-enterologist. "Keone, you had a not-too-rare case of 'the crap.' "

"What's that?"

"You had a back-up in your plumbing. Your sewer was clogged. In short, the mass in your abdomen was nothing more than a deposit of stool. This condition can be caused by anxiety—it's sort of a sophisticated phase of constipation."

I was laughing and rolling on the floor like a maniac, and Keone was yelling indignantly and waving his skinny arms around.

"I spent a hundred dollars on lab tests to find out that I'm constipated? What the hell kind of clinic is this?" He stormed out of the office in search of a rest room. I trailed after him, still laughing.

"Keone, you're full of . . . "

21

The culmination of my second year of medical school was the First Physical Exam. The whole class visited the hospital in the center of town. White-uniformed interns, students, nurses, training nurses, orderlies, and residents were crawling out of the woodwork. Each group of students had as its leader a staff specialist trained extensively in a specific organ system. The group followed the specialist on his rounds, and individual students were often asked to make spur-of-the-moment "diagnoses" on particular patients.

On this day, the sophomore medical class added its contingent, and we were briefed by the Chief of Medicine. We were probably the youngest group touring, and we felt especially distinguished with our black bags, stethoscopes and ophthalmoscopes. We even looked like doctors.

We were paired off in groups of two for the physical examinations. My partner was Keone, who was sure they had paired us so that I could embarrass him in front of the patients.

We were assigned to a patient in the obstetrical ward, a Miss Kathy Downs. The left hand corner of the patient's chart summarized the problem: Miss K. Downs, White, Female, Age 16. Diagnosis: eight weeks pregnant. Planned treatment: therapeutic abortion.

A physical exam performed by a medical student is unlike anything done by a private physician. There are more details, more questions, more listening, more feeling, more peering into orifices, and more trouble keeping the patient patient. Medical students are constantly in fear of overlooking something because they are neophytes.

Avoiding my eyes, Keone said, "I'll take the history and you do the physical." He wanted to do the interview and leave me the body.

"No deal," I replied. "You do the physical." I was very nervous about touching the patient.

We flipped a coin and I lost. I was distressed, not because I minded examining a pretty sixteen-year-old girl, but because I minded examing a *pregnant* sixteen-year-old girl. Besides, I had never done a physical exam before and, despite black bag and stethoscope and reflex hammer that were all brand new and unused (the price tags were still attached), I didn't feel at all like a doctor. I felt like a young, healthy man staring at a young, ripe female body. I would have preferred that my first patient be some blind old lady or unconscious alcoholic.

We walked into the patient's room and were greeted by a tall, muscular 50-year-old gentleman who towered over both of us.

"Well?" he grumbled.

"I am Dr. Goldman and this is Dr. Akana. We're here to give your daughter . . . she is your daughter . . . good . . . we're here to give your daughter a physical before she can be treated."

Keone and I were told to introduce ourselves as

142

"doctor so-and-so." It made the patient feel at ease and it served to make us feel comfortable with a title that would soon be ours for life.

"She's been examined three times," complained Mr. Downs. "What's going on here? Something's wrong. What's the matter? Is she sick? You can tell me, I'm her father."

"Calm down," said Keone. "This is just a part of *our* medical training at this hospital. Don't worry about Kathy."

"*Your* training?" gasped the father. "My daughter's a guinea pig?"

"No, no . . . she's just another patient . . . uh . . . " Keone was at a loss. His explanation didn't satisfy Mr. Downs at all. Soon, the Chief of Medicine came in and took Mr. Downs outside to explain. Kathy had been sitting patiently on the edge of her bed chewing gum and rudely popping bubbles whenever Keone or I spoke.

After her father had been removed, Keone pulled the white curtains around the bed. Kathy was really quite attractive—long blond hair, blue eyes, slender legs, packaged nicely in a pink see-through nightie.

"I see they haven't given you a hospital gown yet," I observed timidly.

"Yeah, they did. I don't wanna wear it. Don't you think this looks better?"

I had to agree with her, but at least the hospital gowns were homely enough to allow the physician some degree of concentration on his job.

Keone started the interview routine. "Ma'am, we have to ask you some routine questions."

"This is the third time today," she frowned.

143

Our recent lectures on "How to Do a Physical" had postulated a rigid series of questions, to be asked in order, about the patient, his or her medical history, the reason for coming to the hospital, and any current problems, including a full summary of "The Present Illness" or condition (in this case) and a complete review of the various bodily systems. The questions are undeniably personal, and many of them are difficult to translate into laymen's terms.

Keone started reading perfunctorily from his index cards.

"Age?"

"Sixteen."

"Sex?"

"What?"

"I mean race."

"What?"

"Marital status?"

"Look!" I broke in. "All that is right here on her chart. Now get to the other stuff." I sat down on a chair next to her bed and waited for Keone to finish his interrogation.

"In your own words, why did you come to the hospital?" asked my roommate. This line of questioning dealt with "The Chief Complaint." It was customary to have the patient himself describe his condition. In this case, however, I thought Keone should have used better judgment.

"Are you nuts?" asked the girl. "Is he nuts?" she repeated, turning to me and pointing her middle finger at Keone. "Why do *you* think I came?"

Keone pressed on. "Describe your present illness."

144

"I'm not sick. I'm pregnant and I'm not married. I didn't come here because I like the scenery."

She must have heard that line in an old Humphrey Bogart movie.

"Keone, let's skip this," I begged. "Ask her about her past medical history."

"Have you had a history of high blood pressure?"

"No."

"Diabetes? Heart disease? Kidney problems?"

"No, to all of them."

"Have you ever been hospitalized before?"

"Yes."

"Well?"

"For tonsils."

"Fine. Have you had all your immunizations?"

Keone was doing very well, and I was impressed. He had put the index cards back into his pocket and was reciting the questions from memory. He asked Kathy Downs about her allergies, whether she had ever been in any accidents, what medication she was presently taking, and whether her family had a high incidence of diabetes or heart disease. He *was* doing very well until he asked about habits.

"Do you take drugs? Do you drink alcohol to excess? Do you smoke cigarettes?" He was firing them so fast I was sure the girl was confused.

"Yes and no," she answered. I was right; she was confused.

"Yes and no?" repeated Keone. He was irritated because the cadence of the interview had been broken.

"Well . . . it's none of your business. I mean, I don't drink or smoke, but it's none of your business, the rest of

145

it." She was staring sullenly at her feet. Since the only other question Keone had asked concerned drugs, he quickly eliminated the other two categories and concentrated on that line of questioning.

"What drugs do you use?" Keone didn't even look up from the chart where he had been marking all this information.

"None of your business."

"Go get her dad," I told Keone.

"Wait! I'll tell you."

"That's better," I nodded, proud of myself.

"Just grass. Honest. Nothing else."

"Okay." said Keone. He pulled the index cards back out of his pocket to locate his place on the questionnaire.

"Now. Lastly, is there a history of cancer in your family?"

"My uncle died of it. Cancer of the lung."

"Okay. And what was his name?"

"Keone!" I shot a glance at him. He was needlessly prolonging this examination to make me suffer.

"Never mind," he continued. "How about strokes?"

"What's a stroke?" asked the girl.

"Never mind," I interrupted, "we can get that information from your father. All right. Now I'm going to do the physical part of this examination. Dr. Akana is through asking you his questions, but I have to ask you some of my own."

"That's okay," she smiled. "You're nicer than he is." She glared at my roommate and stuck out her tongue. Keone snorted and sat down in the chair I had just vacated next to the bed.

146

It was my job to review the systems to see if she was in decent shape before her operation. She looked in fine shape to me, and I was very nervous.

I decided to ask her my questions and examine her simultaneously, although I was doubtful I could do an adequate job of either.

"Have you had any skin problems aside from acne? Any peeling, lesions, that kind of thing? Good." I looked at her fingernails and toenails and then I examined her scalp. "You aren't having any problems with your hair?"

"Yeah, it won't bleach right. It always comes out orange instead of blonde."

"I mean medical. It doesn't fall out in clumps, does it?"

"Nuh-uh."

"Do you bruise easily? Do you bleed excessively? Nose bleeds?"

Kathy Downs just sat there shaking her head. I got out my ophthalmoscope, brand new with brand new batteries, to look into her eyes.

"Follow this light with your eyes," I instructed. "Good."

"How old are you?" she asked suddenly as I was looking at the membranes around her eyes.

"Over twenty," I assured her.

"Do you like being a doctor? Where can I spit this gum?"

"Give it to Dr. Akana. Yeah, I like it."

"Ever seen a dead person?" she asked as I was looking up her nose.

"Yes. Say 'ahhhhh.' Now 'eeeeee.' Now 'oooooooohhhh.' "

147

I checked her gums and her teeth, ignoring the strong bubble-gum odor.

I put away my little flashlight. "Any trouble breathing? At night?" Negative responses. "Any seizures—I mean convulsions, fainting spells, things like that? Very good." I didn't know why I was saying "good" to all her answers, but it sounded very professional.

"Now, do you have any trouble urinating?"

"What?" she looked offended.

"Passing water? Does it burn when you pass water?"

"Oh," she blushed, probably because she didn't catch the meaning of "urinate." "No, never."

"Do you ever have diarrhea?"

"Only after bananas."

"What?" Keone was caught off guard by such a simple answer.

"If I eat more than two bananas a day," she explained.

Now that I was through with her eyes, ears, nose, throat, scalp, hair, fingernails and teeth, I didn't know what to do next. I didn't want to ask her to disrobe. I asked Keone for a consultation.

"We'll be right back," I reassured my patient.

Outside the curtains, I told Keone my problem. "You do her body. You've got more willpower."

"No deal," replied Keone. "She'll probably accuse me of a sex crime just because I look foreign."

We returned to our patient. To stall for time, I checked her neck and underarms for lymph nodes. Fortunately, I didn't find anything, but unfortunately I had to proceed.

148

"Miss Downs... uh... I'm going to ask you to ... well, we've finished the first part of the physical, so now ... "

She interrupted my stammering. "This is taking an awfully long time. Can't we get this over with?"

I turned my back on her and thought of a better way to word the question. When I turned around she was sitting there naked. I let out a short hiccup and motioned for Keone to leave the room. He ignored me. I summoned a nurse, who should be present for legal reasons. Even so, I figured Kathy would be self-conscious with two doctors at her bedside for the examination.

"I don't know what you're waiting for," she muttered. "The first thing those other doctors did was to ask me to take off my clothes."

"Yes, well they were doing a different kind of exam," I explained.

"What?" Keone missed my aside.

"Miss Downs, I'm going to listen to your chest—er, your heart, okay?" I put the stethoscope in my ears and pressed the microphone onto her chest directly between her breasts. I tried not to look but they were so big and beautiful that I actually ignored her heart beat completely for about thirty seconds.

I moved the device around from spot to spot until I landed on her left nipple.

"Not so hard, you're going to kill me!" she squawked, nearly blowing my eardrums out.

I listened all around her back and collarbone and I got kind of comfortable. It was really very nice and her skin was soft. Keone reminded me that it was cold in the room and I had better hurry.

149

"Have you ever had any difficulty with your period?" I asked her. This was a routine series of questions. "When was your first menstrual period?" I was very embarrassed and I was relieved when the girl answered everything quickly and with a minimal amount of comment. "Have you ever had—" I choked.

"What?"

"Ask her, Dr. Akana."

"Ask her what?" queried Keone innocently.

"This is very personal, Miss Downs. Have you ever had venereal disease? Syphilis? Gonorrhea? Crabs?"

I was sweating noticeably and I was tying my stethoscope in knots around my neck.

"No. I never had any of that, thank God!" she giggled.

"Have you ever had any unusual vaginal discharge, especially since you've been pregnant?"

"No," she mused, "I haven't had much of anything since I've been pregnant."

She lay down on the bed as I instructed her and I began going through the four major techniques of cardiovascular and respiratory examination: observation, palpation, percussion, and auscultation. I watched her chest, willingly, for the P.M.I. (point of maximum impulse) where the beating of the heart was externally visible. I found it and showed Kathy, who was unimpressed. I felt around her abdomen for an enlarged liver or spleen, or a distended bladder (this is palpation—feeling). I then tapped her all over her chest, stomach, and back (percussion). This is done to detect any masses whose presence would notably interfere with the

150

normally hollow sound. Finally, I listened to her breathe from the front and the back (auscultation) and concluded that she was perfectly healthy, lung-, heart-, and abdomen-wise.

"You're perfectly healthy up here." It sounded awkward.

"*That* I've heard before." Miss Downs was somewhat of a cynic.

I asked her to sit up and I gave her the nightgown to drape over her body. I examined her joints and tested her reflexes, all of which seemed fine. The physical was over, and it had been more of an ordeal for me than for the pregnant girl.

I let Keone complete the chart. He described the patient (skin, complexion, membranes) and asked a couple more questions. "Have you ever had any psychiatric help?" asked Dr. Akana.

"No. Why? Think I need some?"

"No, no."

I laughed at my roommate from a chair in the corner. I noticed a professor of mine sticking his head in the door. "Hey, Dr. Lennit! Don't I look like a doctor?" I should have kept my mouth shut.

Dr. Lennit smiled. "You sure do, *Mister* Goldman." He disappeared.

Miss Downs grabbed her nightie and covered herself. "*Mister?!*"

"He was only teasing . . . "

"*Mister?!* I've been fondled by a 'mister'?!" Up to that point she had been perfectly willing to let us see every nook and crevice of her wonderful body because she thought we were doctors. In the legal sense, we were *not* doctors. But we had done a professional physical with the sanction of the hospital.

"Wait a second! You have not been 'fondled.' You have been 'examined.' Examined by *Doctor* Akana and myself." I was defending Keone who was cringing in the corner, no doubt worrying about possible criminal charges that might result from doing a routine physical.

"He called you 'mister.' *Daddy!! Daddy!!*"

Keone and I grabbed our black bags and rushed toward the door. It just didn't pay to be a sophomore med student if you couldn't at least *call* yourself a doctor. We collided with Mr. Downs on our way out.

"It's all right, baby," he said. "They're medical students. They know what they're doing. Calm down." He gave us one last scowl as we vanished through the door.

22

Cheryl was coming. Two long years of fantasizing over a pair of pink panties and now—at last—flesh and blood. Cheryl had saved her money until she had accumulated train fare, while her mother, growing impatient with Cheryl's erratic (and infrequent) saving habits, had donated enough bread for a motel room. As far as I was concerned, Mrs. Seltzer should have saved her money— Cheryl wouldn't be using it.

She was coming just in the nick of time. It was the beginning of my junior year in medical school, and I was in a predicament experienced by many single med students. I had been diligent, perhaps too diligent, in my studies. All my friends were male professors and medical students. I knew some women, of course, but only in their professional capacity as doctors, nurses, surgical technicians, or sick people (usually pregnant or dying). I had spent my summers working in Chicago and, during the one week I had visited my home, Cheryl had been in Florida with relatives. I was not only frustrated; I was very lonely.

Mine was the predicament of the single student; married students had their own special problems. A sampling of any med school in the country will probably reveal the same trend: Among those male students who marry in their freshman or their sophomore year of medical school, the divorce rate (after graduation) is considerably higher than the national average. Consciously or unconsciously, lots of guys marry in an attempt to escape the frustration and loneliness inherent in pursuing a medical career. Of course there are other reasons for their getting married, and many couples remain happily wed. But medical school changes a guy. A woman, four years or more into a marriage, may find herself living with a stranger.

First of all, she must learn to endure her husband's neurosis over grades. Secondly, she must accept medicine as a way of life. For some men, the demands of being a doctor may come before the demands of being a husband or father. Even social occasions usually involve spending an evening with other medical students. The wife will probably spend most of these evenings with other wives, while the men discuss medicine. After graduation, things may be worse. A young girl may have had much in common with the young man she married, but four years later their interests may have diverged.

In addition, a medical student is just that—a student. Often, his wife is supporting him, postponing or sacrificing her own career for his. She handles the family finances and makes many decisions without any help from her husband. And she is alone much of the time, while he is on night duty or studying for exams. Both husband and wife must make quite a few adjustments when he finally begins to practice. If the husband assumes the role of provider and decision-maker, many women rebel—asserting their independence. At the other extreme, some women insist on not working at all. They feel that by putting their husbands through med school, they have earned the right to be pampered the rest of their lives. If the husband and wife have never discussed their respective roles, if they can't reach a compromise, their marriage may end in divorce.

None of the philosophical and psychological implications of being a medical student occurred to me when I received Cheryl's letter. The news of her forthcoming visit simply cured me of a severe case of depression. The change in my state of mind was, indeed, remarkable.

"Goldman has finally flipped out. I think he's manic-depressive," Keone announced to the rest of the guys in my house.

"What are the symptoms?" demanded Harvey Durham.

"Well, for weeks he's been walking around here looking like a zombie," replied Keone, "but this morning he was singing and laughing like a maniac. And just now I walked into his room and what did I see? Goldman polishing his black bag with shoe polish!"

My medical history alarmed my roommates, who marched to my room (which I had appropriated when one of my housemates had dropped out of school) to examine the patient for themselves. They found me on my knees surveying my handiwork. My black bag was shining impressively.

"Neat, huh?" I beamed. "Do any of you guys have silver polish?"

"For what, Lloyd?" inquired Keone, rolling his eyes at the others.

"I want to polish my instruments," I replied.

"I'll handle this," said Harvey. Harvey planned to specialize in psychiatry. "Lloyd why do you want to

155

polish your instruments? They're practically brand new."

"I want them to shine," I explained.

"How long have you had this fetish for shiny objects?" asked Harvey gravely.

"Since this morning," I said. I wanted my roommates to share my happiness.

"I told you," said Keone.

"There's still hope," Harvey assured the others. "Don't do anything to upset him. Keone, go find some silver polish." Keone ran off.

"Thanks!" I said. They were really happy for me. "Could I ask you guys for another favor?"

"Anything," Harvey agreed hastily.

"Could you find out if Lee's Laundromat will clean hospital jackets?"

"Hospital jackets?" echoed Harvey. "Lloyd, why don't you just sit down here," he indicated a chair, "and tell us all about hospital jackets."

I was only too happy to oblige. "I'm going to wear them on dates," I explained.

"What dates?" asked Tom Shuler derisively.

Harvey gave him a look of warning. "Tom, go call Lee's," he ordered. Tom obeyed immediately.

My razor-sharp mind sensed that something was amiss. Everyone looked so glum when they should have been so happy.

"Don't you believe me?" I asked Harvey.

"Of course I believe you, Lloyd," he said reassuringly. "I'm sure you'll have plenty of girls."

"No, Harvey," I tried to explain, "just one girl."

"Yes, I know," said Harvey, "and she'll be wonderful and you'll be very happy together."

"She is wonderful, Harvey. You've never seen a body like Cheryl's."

"Cheryl?" Harvey demanded. "Not *the* Cheryl?"

"Who else? She'll be here Friday."

"Why didn't you say so?" Harvey was almost as excited as I was. All my roommates knew about Cheryl. I had even shown them her panties, in a moment of great intimacy, just to prove that she really did exist.

"Tom! Keone!" yelled Harvey. "Cheryl's coming."

They were really happy for me. In fact, I had never seen such exuberance. Harvey and the others caught up with Keone and Tom and everyone began running in circles shouting, "Cheryl's coming!" Keone was babbling in Hawaiian but, for once, he looked happy. There followed an hour of calisthenics and a round of cold showers before any of us even approached a state conducive to sleep that night. Now that I think about it, cold showers were in great demand all the rest of that week.

During this time, I was busy planning. I wanted everything to be just right, so I decided to order some flowers for Cheryl and have them waiting at the house when we returned from the station. The florist said the only way I could get them in time was to pick them up myself on Friday afternoon. It was a long drive and I was pressed for time, but I refused to abandon the flower plan.

I sped along the Chicago Skyway, my black bag and stethoscope on the front seat in case a patrolman tried to stop me for speeding. A dozen red roses were waiting for me at the florist—traditional but effective. I

157

laid the bouquet gently on the back seat and started speeding home to a waiting vase.

Without warning, the traffic began to get thicker and thicker. My progress slowed to a crawl. Infuriated, I leaned on the horn and began yelling ugly things out the window at no one in particular, who began yelling even uglier things back at me. My anger evaporated when I saw the flashing red light. I knew that my responsibility—even as a medical student—was to help.

From a half-mile away, I could see that it was a bad accident with several cars involved. There was no ambulance, just one police car. One patrolman was directing traffic around the accident while his partner was struggling with limp bodies among the wreckage.

I steered my Pontiac out of the mainstream and onto the grass plateau bordering the highway. I parked next to the police car.

"I'm a doctor," I lied. I wasn't sure anymore. I knew what to do in emergency situations even though I wasn't really a doctor yet. But I didn't want to bore the cop with my story and I didn't want the victims to bleed to death, so I just hopped out of the car with my black bag and headed toward the injured.

There were six victims in all. One, a small boy, was dead. He had gone right through the windshield and had probably died instantly on impact. The other five were all adults, all badly lacerated, and all conscious.

It was an unpleasant scene—a lot of crying and moaning and blood. The blood I had learned to live with; the crying and moaning terrified me, and I felt like running. I had never been in a situation like this and I felt a terrible burden of responsibility.

One of the victims, a young woman, had just been pulled from a car by a policeman. She was in bad shape but conscious. Her leg was badly broken, and I had to get a splint somewhere. None of the policemen had any ideas so I appropriated one of their billy clubs to use in setting the bone. When I returned to the girl she had lapsed into unconsciousness. I felt a sense of relief, knowing she wouldn't feel the pain.

I set the leg without difficulty, although in my courses I had always had a hard time setting broken bones. The tension of being in a crisis situation helped my performance. To my surprise, I worked well under pressure.

"Where the hell is that ambulance?" I demanded. It had been about fifteen minutes since I arrived, time enough for another doctor to join me. He pulled up in a new Lincoln and parked right next to my old Pontiac.

I was running out of gauze and iodine and xylocaine when I saw a wrecker pull up. Still no ambulance, but the damn wrecker was all ready to start dragging the cars away from the scene.

About ten minutes passed before *real* help arrived— two ambulances. Even then, my work wasn't finished until all the bodies, living and dead, had been loaded into the ambulances and taken away.

Dazed and feeling weak, I started walking slowly in the direction of my Pontiac. It was a few seconds before I noticed my car was not where I had left it.

"Where is my car?" I asked the only remaining cop, who was sitting on his motorcycle filling out the report.

"Who are you?" he shot back at me.

"I'm a doctor. I've been here for half an hour helping these people."

"Oh, yeah," he nodded without looking up. "Thanks for stopping. Real mess, huh?"

"Where's my car?"

"I dunno. What'd it look like? Maybe it was stolen."

"Maroon Pontiac. It was parked right over there."

"Oh," chuckled the cop, "was that thing yours?"

"What do you mean, 'was'?" I asked, fearing the worst.

"Well, I thought it was one of the cars in the wreck. I told the wrecker to haul it off."

"What?!" I screamed. The cop just smiled.

"You can pick it up down at headquarters. We won't even charge you for towing."

I had one hour before Cheryl's train was due to arrive. The police station was on the opposite side of town. I knew I could never get my car back and return to the train station in an hour, but I was going to try.

"Can you take me to the police station?" I asked the cop.

"Sure," he replied. "Hop on."

All the way to the station, I was balanced precariously on the back of the motorcycle, clutching my black bag and stethoscope in one hand and hanging on to the cop with the other. I felt slightly nauseous as I stumbled into the station thirty minutes later.

Claiming my car was no easy task. Getting out of paying the towing charges was even more difficult. Then I had to talk the desk sergeant into giving me back my roses. He had taken them to give to his girl friend. I also tried to talk him into giving me a police escort to the train station, but no dice.

I was forty-five minutes late when I finally pulled into the station. I grabbed the roses and dashed inside where I was directed to Gate 29. Gate 29 was deserted except for a few lone travelers scattered around the waiting area. Cheryl was not among them. I was frantic.

She could be anywhere, I thought. Knowing Cheryl, she ran off with the conductor.

My thoughts were interrupted by one of the travelers, a chick with long, frizzy, tangled hair.

"Hi!" she said with a smile.

I glanced at her. I didn't know any freaky-looking chicks. Just my luck. For once in my life a girl tries to pick *me* up and I'm going crazy trying to find my date, who probably would be much happier if I never showed up.

"Lloyd!" persisted the strange girl.

I peered more closely. Then I gasped, feeling as if someone had socked me in the stomach. There could be no mistaking that body.

"Cheryl!" I squeaked.

"Hi, Lloyd," she repeated, beaming.

"My God, Cheryl. What have they done to you?" I gasped again. I couldn't believe my eyes. This couldn't be Cheryl Seltzer of Saks wardrobe fame. This couldn't be the same girl who wore makeup to bed. This imposter was clad only in a T-shirt and jeans. Her face was devoid of makeup, and her hair was cascading wildly in all directions. Only the body remained the same, but all the more provocative (if possible) because now it was braless.

Cheryl spotted the roses. "Lloyd, what's that?" she cried.

161

Still dazed, I muttered, "They're roses."

"Oh, Lloyd, how sweet!" Cheryl, who had probably already received more roses in her short lifetime than I'll ever see in mine, seemed genuinely moved.

Of course, I had planned everything I would say when we met. Now I was so stunned, I could only stare at her, open-mouthed.

"I'm hungry," Cheryl announced. "Is there a health food restaurant nearby? Let's go."

This was a far cry from the elegant French restaurants of Washington.

Over dinner, Cheryl told me how a guy she had dated had "turned her on to self-fulfillment." Although the guy had split, Cheryl had stayed turned on. At the moment she was "into" the feminist movement.

"My head's straight now, Lloyd," she assured me.

Her mother was "into" psychiatric analysis trying to get her own head straight after what Cheryl's transformation had done to it.

Cheryl insisted on paying her share of the check. My amazement over the change in her character was giving way to admiration.

When we arrived back at the house, there was a welcoming committee consisting of my roommates. Everyone wanted to meet Cheryl and everyone failed to recognize her from the description I had given. After the introductions, Cheryl was given a tour of the house. The tour stopped abruptly at Tom Shuler's room. Tom had the most extensive nude poster collection in the school.

"What's this?" Cheryl asked.

"It's my poster collection. What of it?" Tom was on the defensive.

162

"It seems to me a junior medical student would have better things to do with his time," Cheryl remarked cryptically. Then she turned and abruptly left the room. Tom looked stunned and embarrassed, while the rest of us shifted uneasily.

In spite of Cheryl's anti-sexist philosophy, her voluptuous body was making me incredibly horny. I was forced to endure cruel and unusual punishment when we adjourned to my room so she could practice her yoga exercises. A half hour later she was in the supine position of relaxation. I was in an equally supine position, collapsed across my bed, limp with frustration and exhaustion.

Oh, cruel irony. This was the moment I had been dreaming of. Cheryl, myself, a bed, a locked door. Only now if I even tried to touch her, she would denounce me as a sexist.

"Well?" Cheryl interrupted my reverie.

"Well what?" I asked, bewildered.

"Let's not play games, Lloyd," she said. "We've been doing that long enough. It's perfectly natural for a man and a woman to be together."

"You mean . . . ?"

"Yes!"

"But . . . do you think we should?"

"Yes!"

"But . . . your mother."

"What's she got to do with it?"

"Well then . . . my mother."

"Lloyd, you're a big boy now, and I've been attracted to you for a long time."

"You have??!!"

163

"Of course. You're a beautiful person, Lloyd."

I must be dreaming, I thought. I pinched myself. I wasn't dreaming. Now, after years of planning and scheming for this very moment, I was helpless. Throughout all those years of grade-grubbing, neurosis, self-doubt, and endurance, Cheryl had remained the object of my desires. She was a goal, just as an M.D. was a goal. Only I had thought of her as something to be enjoyed, to be had physically. Now, emotions had entered the picture. Cheryl had changed, and I liked her. She was independent of her mother's thinking, now. She was unpretentious and unpredictable. And she was someone I could talk to. I liked her, and I was afraid to let her see just how much I liked her.

Perhaps sensing my fear, Cheryl came over and sat next to me on the bed. I was afraid to move. After a few minutes, I could feel her hands creeping under my shirt. Her cold finger-tips made circles on my chest. Her hands gradually warmed and she slowly unbuttoned my shirt. Her soft lips touched my neck.

I relaxed as she gently caressed my naked back. The warmth of her breasts pressing against my chest sent an electrical impulse through my body. I held Cheryl as tightly as I could. For the first time in the past two years, my mind was free from medicine . . .

Waking before dawn with Cheryl in my arms was unlike anything I had ever dreamed. We talked until morning, reminiscing about the past few years.

"Do you know how many years I've waited, Cheryl?"

"I *know,* Lloyd," she giggled. "I remember our first dinner together—with my parents. You were so

164

nervous. And my mother wouldn't leave you alone. I felt terrible."

"No you didn't. You enjoyed every minute of it."

"I guess I did," Cheryl laughed.

"And what about the time you came on so strong and then took off with that cop?"

"He forgot your ticket, didn't he?" she teased. "Seriously, Lloyd, all through those years both of us were playing on each other's weaknesses. We weren't really being ourselves. I was a robot, programmed by my mother since the day I was born. I was responding to a fantasy—the doctor image. And society channeled your thinking too—a good lay."

My body stiffened. Every one of my muscles contracted.

"Lloyd, don't misunderstand. I'm not being critical. Any normal male who is exposed to a bikini torture at the time his male hormones are at peak level would react the same way. All that is simple, natural, superficial human behavior. But, there is something deeper about you, something more profound which surfaces every once in a while. That's the real Lloyd—the one I respect."

I fell back to sleep knowing that I loved Cheryl Seltzer.

23

I wanted Cheryl to see that medical school was not just textbooks—that there was a great deal of clinical experience and plenty of contact with real human beings. On Saturday morning, I brought her to the hospital.

"I want you to meet some of the patients, Cheryl," I explained. "Having visitors does a lot for their morale."

When we entered the hospital, I spotted a doctor I knew and stopped to discuss a patient in whom I had a personal interest. I was so engrossed in the conversation, I completely forgot about Cheryl. When I returned to where I had left her, she was gone. I found her at the admissions desk.

"What's up Cheryl?" I asked, coming up beside her.

"This poor man," she said, indicating a sickly old fellow, "has been waiting almost five hours to see a doctor. All he wants are pain pills for his arthritis and so far he's had to wait in four different lines—for his hospital card, his appointment schedule, his medical record, and his X-rays! On top of that he's diabetic and he's had to skip breakfast and lunch. When he does get in, he'll probably spend a whole five minutes with some doctor he's never seen before."

"Don't be upset, Cheryl," I said. "If he were in immediate danger, he'd be in the emergency room. Why don't we go have a cup of coffee before we visit the patients?"

I tried to cheer her up over coffee, but she had been deeply affected by the old man's plight. She lectured me for a half hour on the difficulty of gaining access to health care in an inner city hospital.

I was afraid her low spirits would affect the patients, but she had regained her self-control by the time we reached the ward. I had been assigned to five patients in my physical diagnosis course, and Cheryl accompanied me on my rounds. One of the patients was a man with kidney failure. Because he was a diabetic, with many associated complications, he wasn't a candidate for a dialysis machine (artificial kidney treatment) and had less than a month to live. His wife and eldest child were waiting outside when we left the patient. I related his medical history to Cheryl, explaining in lay terminology the physiology of renal failure. I was trying to make it clear to Cheryl that the intern in charge was doing everything he could to prolong the man's life by regulating his blood chemistries.

"Can the intern save his life?" Cheryl asked, matter-of-factly.

"Well . . . no . . . it's not possible, but we're doing all we can."

"Are you sure, Lloyd?" Cheryl asked. "What about his family? Is there anyone to provide for them when he's gone? Couldn't the hospital send a social worker to find out?"

Of course, I should have thought of that. I had

been so wrapped up in the academic side of this man's illness—in why we *couldn't* help him—that I had overlooked a very simple and practical way in which we *could* help.

By now, I was really hung on Cheryl. She was no longer the irresponsible and self-centered girl I had known. I had never thought it possible for someone to change so completely.

Cheryl's visit was not trouble-free, however. Before leaving the clinic, I had some errands to run. Cheryl waited in a lounge which was a favorite hangout of med students' wives. When I returned thirty minutes later I found her deep in discussion with Mary Ellen Taylor, the wife of my friend Bob.

"You're right, Cheryl," Mary Ellen was saying as I approached them. "I never thought of it that way."

"What's that?" I asked politely.

"Bob's very oppressive," replied Mary Ellen.

I was sorry I asked.

"Lloyd," Cheryl said. "Did you know that Mary Ellen dropped out of school to finance her husband's education?"

"Oh, really?" I replied. All of this struck me as terribly personal.

"Yes," asserted Mary Ellen, "and now Bob treats me like a maid. Being married to Bob is no better than babysitting. I'm going to take your advice, Cheryl. Things will be different from now on."

"We have to go now," I interrupted. I was getting nervous. Bob was my friend.

"Just remember," Cheryl called out as I grabbed her arm and started pulling her away, "everything he has he owes to you . . . "

169

By now I had dragged Cheryl out the door. My sigh of relief was short-lived, however. There coming up the steps was Bob Taylor.

"Goldman," he called in greeting.

"Hi," I said trying to slip past him.

"Hey, aren't you going to introduce me to your friend?"

"Cheryl," I said begrudgingly, "this is a friend of mine."

"What's wrong, Goldman? Afraid someone's going to steal her away? I'm Bob Taylor, Cheryl."

"Oh! Why, I was just talking to your wife."

"Say, maybe the four of us can get together tonight. I'll give you a call, Goldman."

"Sure, Bob," I said, knowing that was one phone call I'd never receive.

I spent the rest of the afternoon showing Cheryl the Chagall mosaic and Picasso sculpture in the center of Chicago and keeping her as far away from the medical school as possible. Even if Bob never spoke to me again, I really couldn't blame Cheryl. She had merely discovered one of the most serious problems facing medical students and their families. The demands of a medical career are not placed solely on the med student or M.D. Wives and families often find themselves playing second fiddle to a very demanding profession.

The weekend flew by, and Sunday night and Cheryl's departure time rolled around. I had been in a state of bliss for three days, rejoicing in Cheryl's transformation.

"Cheryl," I said, as we joined the line of passengers waiting to board her train, "you've got to come again soon. I can't wait another two years."

"Neither can I, Lloyd," she said. "I'll be back—soon." I kissed her goodbye and watched until her train pulled out of the station. Then I drove home, still meditating on how much Cheryl had changed. Back at the house I went directly to my room in order to be alone and think about Cheryl. I lay across the bed, my head propped on the pillow, my eyes wandering aimlessly about the room. Suddenly, my eyes riveted to the dresser. There, wrapped neatly around my can of shaving cream was something fluffy and soft. My feet hadn't touched the ground, but I found myself at my dresser, clutching the panties in my hands. There it was again—a bold, clear number "one." I laughed out loud, recalling the day, two years earlier, when I had found the first pair of panties. At that time, Cheryl Seltzer had symbolized just one thing—physical fulfillment. When I considered her character, which was seldom, I thought of her as her mother's daughter—selfish, man-chasing, and not too bright. Now, I recalled that she had often laughed at her mother. Had the other Cheryl been simply a product of my own perception? Not entirely, but I hadn't been concerned with discovering the woman Cheryl might become.

My eyes returned to the panties I still clutched in my hand and my mind whirled joyously as I thought of the infinite possibilities symbolized by the number "one."

24

My third year of med school was filled with initiations into the mechanics of medicine: my first delivery, my first appendectomy, my first experience in the operating room with a scalpel in my hand. Every new adventure was as thrilling as it was terrifying. All the textbooks and all the lectures were forgotten the minute an emergency came up.

"Delivery! Deeelivery!" Two orderlies were rushing a stretcher down the corridor. I was in the prep room examining a woman who was six months pregnant and experiencing back pain. One of the orderlies stuck his head in and asked for help. "Doctor, we've got a lady out here who's ready to go."

"Oh . . . well," I gave up and followed them down the hall, leaving my half-naked patient on the table.

"Are you the resident?" asked the orderly. "An intern? A male nurse? A midwife?"

"I'm a medical student."

"Good. Wash up. Hurry!"

I wondered why I was taking orders from an orderly, but there was no time to argue. When we got to the delivery room, I flipped up the sheet on the woman. The orderly was right. The head had already appeared at the vaginal opening. I rushed outside to wash up; I had time for no more than a quick soap and water job, like I used to do before dinner at home. I put on the blue surgical garb which covered me from my hair to my shoes and rushed back into Delivery. The woman was obviously in a great deal of pain and the knowledge that she was depending on me to relieve that pain intensified my nervousness. I tried desperately to think of the mnemonics for deliveries:

"P" stood for prep—scrub the mother down with disinfectant. "D" stood for drape—cover the patient with the obstetrical sheets. "M" was for the maneuvers that the doctor has to go through the minute the baby's head exits—he must rotate the child so that the shoulders and rest of the body follow smoothly. "C" meant clamp and snip—for the umbilical cord. There was also a letter "S" that stood for something, no doubt important, but I couldn't remember what it was.

"What does 'S' stand for?" I asked a nurse.

She grabbed me by the hand and dragged me outside to the scrub area. "You've got some time. Go ahead and scrub," she ordered.

I started cleaning my nails. "What does the 'S' mean?" I repeated.

"What are you talking about?"

"You know: P.D.M.C.S. The formula. That's how we were taught to remember what to do in delivery. I can't remember the 'S.'"

"Well, I haven't got the faintest idea. Use more soap," ordered my unfriendly old nurse as she scowled over my shoulder. "Now, why did you turn the faucets off with you hand?"

In my haste, I had recontaminated my hands by touching the faucets instead of using my elbows. I apologized and started to rewash.

174

"Forget it. No time." Back through the swinging doors we went. The surgical gloves looked quite impressive on *my* hands.

The groaning woman was having contractions, and I approached the table like a jet to a runway. An aide was directing me into a white sterile garment.

"Hands up, doctor. Below the waist and you're contaminated."

"What?" I raised my hands, expecting to be frisked.

"If you touch yourself below the waist now, you'll have to rewash." The aide helped me get into my surgical garb. In doing so she loosened my trousers. She had been trying to tie the surgical garment and she had *untied* the front of my already-baggy hospital pants which immediately began to drop. If I pulled them up, I would be contaminated again.

"Hurry, doctor. Here comes the head." Sure enough, the red, round little bubble was slowly emerging from the shaven pudendal region. I leaned up against the table, stopping the trousers from descending any further. I splashed the disinfecting prep all over the legs and abdomen of the mother, who groaned louder.

"Lloyd, Lloyd!!" moaned the lady on the table.

I blanched and jumped back. My pants started slipping again. "Don't worry," said a nurse. "That's her husband's name."

I remembered the "D for drape" step and I ordered one of the nurses to get the sterile sheets in place. I saw the eyes of the infant as more and more of the head became visible. I was handed a needle, five inches long.

It was time to anesthetize the patient. I had just taken a pop quiz on anesthetization a month earlier but had forgotten most of it. However, I distinctly remembered the landmarks—where to aim for killing pain in the female groin. The only problem was that this woman was writhing in agony and calling a name that her husband and I had in common. The problem was compounded by the baby's head, which was now obscuring the target area.

Fortunately, this woman was a multipara; that is, she had delivered several babies before. She was 6-6-0-6 (six full term infants, six pregnancies, zero abortions, and six living children). The birth canal was accommodating this infant quite adequately and I saw no need to do an episiotomy on her.

My trousers were now down around my ankles, the student nurse was staring at my bare legs and underwear, and I was having just one hell of a time concentrating. My mind was in chaos. I was still worried about "S" and whatever that meant. Somehow, I got the needle in and pushed the plunger, reasonably sure that I was within an inch or two of the nerve.

As I withdrew the needle, the baby's head popped out completely. I grabbed the rubber suction bulb and cleared the mouth of any mucous. The baby let out a loud yell (the louder the better), and I felt slightly relieved.

I rotated the body and twisted and pulled until I freed the shoulders. After that, the little creature slid right out into my hands, slippery as hell and genuinely ugly. I had a feeling that I was going to drop the baby, a little girl, so I tried to get a better grip. Since the little thing was so slimy, I lost what little hold I had had on her and started juggling the infant around. The baby was

176

screaming, and the old nurse who had been scolding me earlier was screaming (in laughter) as she pointed at my half-naked torso. It was bad enough that my pants were down in front of a half-dozen nurses, none of whom had the dignity to ignore the predicament, but to be seen bouncing a newborn from one hand to the other almost surely qualified me for expulsion from the delivery room. I was finally handed a towel.

I secured a couple of clamps on the umbilical cord and snipped between the two so that the baby was finally unattached. The aides and the nurses began washing the child and daubing its eyes with silver nitrate. I was standing there, my hands at my sides, trying to recover from all the screaming. P.D.M.C.S. All that rote memory in med school paid off.

The baby was handed back to me and, as a gesture of friendship, I wobbled up to the head of the table.

"Look! A new baby girl!" I held the squinting, red, moist little body up where the mother could see it. Instead of the traditional and expected maternal smile, Lloyd's wife turned her head away.

"Ohhh no. Ohhh no!" she wailed.

"What's the matter with you?" I demanded. "This is a beautiful thing. It's been hard work for all of us."

"I have six girls at home," she cried, "and my husband wanted a little boy. We've been trying for a little boy for eight years."

I turned to one of the nurses, who could see I was perturbed but who continued to laugh at the pants around my ankles. I handed the baby to the nurse and gracefully leaned over and pulled up my pants.

"Lloyd! Ohhh!" moaned the lady on the table.

177

" 'Six girls and I wanted a boy! ' " I mimicked as I stalked out of the delivery room.

Outside, I started peeling off the shoe covers, the mask, and the hood for my hair. The old nurse appeared through the swinging doors.

"You made a real spectacle of yourself in there," she said. She just had to remind me. "But that was an excellent delivery. Good job." She hit me on the shoulder like a marine sergeant. I was very grateful for the compliment.

"Thanks. I was nervous."

"*You* were nervous? How do you think *I* felt when you almost dropped that little girl on her soft little skull?" She chuckled heartily.

"Yeah, that was close," I muttered. "Hey, have you been able to remember what 'S' means?"

The old nurse glared at me. "You and your damn formulas. 'S' in my book means 'shit' and nothing more. Forget the formula, will ya? You did everything right. Isn't that enough?"

"Yes ma'am," I nodded in mock respect. "It sure is. But I imagine Dr. Schroeder would kill me if I forgot his clever P.D.M.C.S."

"Forget Dr. Schroeder," said the old nurse. "He fainted during *his* first delivery. Fainted—do you believe that?"

25

Pediatrics was my next stop on the clinical rotation that would continue well into my senior year of medical school. I was assigned three on-service patients, children who had been in the hospital for a while.

Charlene was my favorite. She was a spunky three-year-old black girl who had been in perfect health until two weeks before, when she had suffered a grand mal seizure. The cause of this episode was attributed to hypoglycemia (low sugar in the blood). Upon her arrival at the hospital, the resident had given her intravenous glucose, and the activity had quickly subsided. She had spent the last two weeks undergoing extensive (and expensive) workups to determine the cause of her bouts with hypoglycemia. About all that was really accomplished during this time was that the considerations had been reduced to possible sensitivity to a certain diet, in-born liver damage, or merely an early manifestation of diabetes.

Charlene started crying the minute I walked into her room for the first time. My hospital jacket symbolized more needles, more tubes in her arm, and more pain.

"I'm not going to stick you, Charlene. Honest. I just want to listen to your heart."

The sobbing continued, and the little girl turned over and faced the window next to her bed.

I had come completely prepared, or so I thought. I opened my black bag to a wide assortment of candies. "How about a candy cane?"

Charlene's crying got louder.

"OK, OK." I patted her shoulder. "Here, how about a Mars bar? No? What's the matter?" I sifted through piles of candy bars and lollipops, looking for something out of the ordinary that might please the little girl. "Here, try this." I opened her little clenched fist and filled her hand with some jelly beans.

"Yuk. I want Mommy." She threw the jelly beans on the floor and continued wailing. I rang for a nurse.

"What's the matter with this kid?" I demanded, taking the nurse out into the corridor. "She's scared to death. I try to give her candy, and she screams louder. What's happened to her?"

The nurse just shook her head and motioned for me to follow her. She reentered Charlene's room and retrieved a shoe box from under the bed. "Open it."

Inside was a collection of candy and sweets and bubble gum that would have made a trick-or-treater drool enviously. My cohorts had beaten me to the punch, and Charlene was obviously sick to death of candy: candy equals doctor; doctor equals needles; needles equal pain.

"I'm sorry," I told the nurse. She turned up her nose and walked out.

I sat on the edge of Charlene's bed. "Listen, Charlene, have you ever played with one of these?" I took out my stethoscope. Her huge eyes stared suspiciously at me over her shoulder. Then she turned around to face me. I plugged the earphones into her ears and

180

placed the other end over my heart, slipping the diaphragm under my hospital jacket so that she could hear the beating clearly.

A smile crept across her moist little face, and the sniffling stopped shortly thereafter. I let her listen to my heart and lungs for about five minutes before continuing the strategy.

"My turn. My turn, Charlene." I tried to indicate that I was going to listen to *her* for a while. This was difficult to communicate—every time I started to speak the little girl squealed. I was blowing her eardrums out.

Finally, with sign language, I got the message across. She responded, in sign language, by shaking her head.

"No, no. I wanna play." She grinned at me.

"Charlene, listen to me." I removed the listening end of the stethoscope from my chest and covered it with my hand so I wouldn't hurt her ears. "I am the doctor. I'm not going to hurt you. I want to listen to *you*, now. You've had your turn. OK?" I was in a hurry because I was scheduled to present this case to the chairman of the Department of Pediatrics in thirty minutes. Charlene was wasting a good bit of that time arguing with me.

I reached into my bag and came up with my new ophthalmoscope, the instrument used for eye examination. While Charlene was listening to my hand, I turned on the light in this gadget and tried to get a decent look at the back of her eye. If there was diabetes, it could possibly show up. Such an examination could also reveal brain tumors, internal bleeding in the skull, high blood pressure, or ordinary damage to the optic nerve and

181

retina. Nothing was certain in this girl's diagnosis so I felt that I might, indeed, learn something from her eyes.

Charlene shut her eyes immediately. When she did, I instantly (and gently) reclaimed my stethoscope. She opened her eyes again and started crying. To make up for her lost toy, I decided to give her my reflex hammer (the ophthalmoscope was too expensive for a three-year-old's touch). She started pounding on my hands and legs and shoulders, laughing hysterically.

"You've got to quiet down." I couldn't hear a thing in her chest if she was laughing and thrashing around. "Please, honey, just for a minute." My time was running out, and I didn't know what I was going to tell the chairman of Pediatrics about this girl.

The girl became silent suddenly. "That's good." The heartbeat was coming in loud and clear. Charlene picked up the bell of the stethoscope.

"Doctor? *Doctor?* Can you hear me?"

My eardrums vibrated viciously in my skull. "What? What's that?"

Charlene's mother was standing next to the bed. "Have you found anything? She's been in here two weeks, now."

I took off the stethoscope. "I'm brand new here," I explained, "and I have to do a physical on your daughter and get a report to one of my superiors in fifteen minutes. Do you think you can calm her down a little?"

"You want me to spank her?" asked the well-meaning mother.

"*No!* Just ask her to be still. I know she's been through a lot lately."

Charlene and her mother talked privately for a few minutes while I visited Charlene's roommate, another little girl, the victim of an auto accident who was strung up in a maze of ropes, apparently in traction. I gave her my whole supply of candy before leaving. She smiled appreciatively.

"Doctor, she's ready."

"Thank you, Mrs. Weaver."

I raced through the physical in the final ten minutes and finished just in time for the case presentation. After my meeting with the chairman of the department, Mrs. Weaver asked to see me again.

Charlene's mother was worried, and justifiably so, about the lack of progress her daughter had been making since entering the hospital. Two weeks ago she had a healthy little girl, and now her daughter was experiencing regular seizures.

"They haven't found out what's wrong yet?"

"No. I'm just a medical student. The intern knows the whole story." I felt sorry for her because I knew that the hospital bills were going to keep her family in debt for years after Charlene's problems were resolved in the hospital.

The next day when I went to visit Charlene, her mother was in the room.

"Oh, good," said the little girl, grabbing my stethoscope to repeat our game.

I unbuttoned my coat again so she could listen to my heart.

"No, no!"

"Don't you want to play today?"

"No!" said Charlene, "not with you. Today let's

listen to Mommie's heart." She started unbuttoning her mother's blouse. I looked away quickly.

"No, honey," said her mother, "that's the doctor's job. Mommie's doctor. Dr. Goldman is Charlene's doctor." After a brief exchange Mrs. Weaver convinced her daughter that I was the one who should do the auscultating today . . . .

Pediatrics was not much fun for me. If nothing else, it gave me a deep respect for pediatricians because they are probably the most patient people on earth. For four weeks I had my fill of five-month-old infants running at the rectum, ten-year-old busters running at the nose, and twenty-year-old debutantes running at the mouth. It is a diarrheic profession, in every sense of the word.

The newborn nursery, the other part of my pediatrics duty, was fun for the first couple of days. But like everything else in pediatrics, it turned sour after a while. Junior med students were a vital part of the evaluation crew. Every morning a new truckload of babies was transported to the nursery for fueling, vehicle inspection, and general maintenance. We were given a checklist to use. Keone and I were usually paired together and we alternated roles as the inspector and the recorder.

"Toes?" asked Keone.

"Ten," I would usually report after checking. A couple of the babies would have one or two extra.

"Fingers?"

"Ten."

"Appendages?" Keone continued right on down the list.

The usual place for appendages was on the tips of the ears, and the treatment was simple. A string was tied tightly around the base of the structure which would invariably fall off in a week or so without infection or pain to the infant.

Next on the list was respiration. Could the baby breathe through his mouth? (I held his nose to check.) Through his nose? (I put my hand over his mouth.)

"Rectum?" called out Keone, completing the basic inventory.

The report on rectums was usually positive; that is, there usually *was* a rectum. In any event, there was only one way to find out if there was an orifice and that was to stick your finger up there. There are a few rare but true stories about pediatricians and residents who spent days trying to determine why an infant vomited constantly or suffered from a distended abdomen and never passed waste. Finally, after numerous blood tests and X-rays, it came to light that the evaluation team had forgotten to notice that the baby in basinette twelve was rectumless—that is, one sliver of skin was blocking traffic. Otherwise, all systems were "go."

One day, when I was the recorder, we ran across such a case.

"Rectum?" I called out.

"Negative, I think," reported Keone in an unusually uncertain tone of voice. "I think this one is plugged up." Keone's amazement stemmed from the fact that he had, in a spare moment, looked up the statistics for rectumless infants and found them to be amazingly scarce in the United States. "This is something," he whistled.

185

Keone lifted the baby up for a closer look. "No rectum!"

We reported the condition to the resident who commended both of us for our evaluation. "This could have been real trouble had you missed it," he said. "Last year we had a newborn that weighed 12 pounds after two weeks. Ate like a son-of-a-bitch. Just couldn't crap at all!"

I was happy to learn that a simple incision remedied this painful condition.

After a while, the newborn nursery began to bore me. The only thing that was keeping me from deserting the pediatrics ward was Charlene, my one bright spot in days filled with bubble gum and acrid diapers and slobbering. We developed a friendship; she was quite a conversationalist. Her seizures, however, were as yet unsolved. Her mother was frantic. Relatives poured in and out of her room all day long.

There wasn't anything I could do besides the routine examinations. The tests were showing up absolutely nothing. My only consolation was in the fact that we were regulating the hypoglycemic episodes with diet.

During my fourth week in pediatrics, I was doing nursery duty early in the morning when one of the pediatricians came in.

"Dr. Goldman? You better come on down here."

"What's the matter?"

"The Weaver girl had another seizure during the night. A bad one."

"Did she come out of it?" My voice cracked pitifully.

186

"Well, she came to after the attack and seemed to be recovering nicely. That was about 3 a.m. The nurses were checking her regularly after that until this morning."

"She died?"

"Yeah. In her sleep around 6 a.m. Hypoglycemic shock. The family is outside now. They want to see her. The nurses said you were on the case."

"I'll tell them. Thanks for letting me know."

In somewhat of a trance and with my teeth grinding to dust, I marched down the corridor to Charlene's room. Her body had already been removed. I saw Mr. and Mrs. Weaver and the grandmother; there were two small children running around the halls playing tag. We had been briefed by psychiatrists on telling a family that a "loved one" had passed away. There were all sorts of euphemisms. I was trying desperately to recall the simplest and most painless. At the same time, I was fighting my own grief coupled with a feeling of bitterness directed toward a hospital that keeps a little girl for a month and then buries her with no progress at all.

Mrs. Weaver approached me.

"Dr. Goldman, they won't let me see her. I'm her mother. Please! I know something is wrong. Let me see my baby!" She was starting to cry, and I think she knew then that Charlene was dead. Her husband put his arms around her and looked at me expectantly.

"Uhm. Sit down, won't you?" I moved to a bench in the corridor and the whole family clustered around me. My memory returned and I started the routine. We had been told in class that we should waste no time.

187

My eyes were misty and my hands were sweating. "Charlene . . . died this morning." Mrs. Weaver let out a short cry and buried her head in her husband's shoulder.

"I'm very sorry. I really am. You did *everything* you could do. She fought hard . . . she was a strong little girl. You did everything you could do. She had the best possible medical attention." Bullshit. I was very angry with the whole profession. I was struggling very hard not to break down myself, an act which is strongly discouraged by fellow professionals.

The whole family was crying now. I put my arms around Mrs. Weaver and then moved down the corridor back to the nursery. Five minutes of mourning. That was what our psychiatry lecturer had suggested. Then, you can ask for an autopsy.

My head was aching. I didn't want to ask that family for anything. I wanted to run away from that place. Four weeks and no one knew what was wrong with that girl. A three-year old body can endure only so much.

I left the Weavers alone for ten full minutes before returning, this time a little more composed.

"I am truly sorry," I repeated. "You know what good friends Charlene and I had become. She was in no pain at all."

Mrs. Weaver nodded her head. "You've been so helpful, doctor. We had our doubts . . . you know? I mean when she was sick for so long and no one could give us any answers . . . we just figured she might die, you know?"

"There are no answers," I said, fully realizing, for the first time, that medicine can't cure everyone. "I

188

wish there were, but there just aren't right now. I know that Charlene will live on in the memories of all her loved ones. I can't remember when I've seen such a kind, warm family who spent so much time with a patient." This was standard in the routine, but I really meant it. The only thing that had kept that little girl in good spirits was the constant influx of visiting relatives.

"Mrs. Weaver . . . uh," I was stammering, but I knew that I'd have to say it. "We need your permission to do an autopsy. It is for the sake of medical science and it would help us determine what is wrong with Charlene, *was* wrong, and then we could help others with her condition."

I finished the whole speech as quickly as I could, emphasizing nothing and speaking in an undertone.

"No, Doctor, please!" Mr. Weaver told me that he didn't want the hospital to touch Charlene's body again. It was a religious principle—he wanted God to be the next and last person to take Charlene. Under the circumstances, I could not argue. I did feel concerned from a medical point of view. A post mortem exam is useful especially when the diagnosis is unknown. I wanted to find out what was wrong. On the other hand, I knew what an autopsy involved and was relieved when Mr. Weaver refused.

I said good-bye to the Weavers, instructing them to stop by the cashier's desk for a final invoice on the way out. Hospitalization is an industry; people come in and go out on a financial note. The very poor can qualify for free medical care (if they can find it). The very rich can afford the very best. The hard-working middle-class family is stuck in the middle, and the burdens of a long hospital stay linger with the pocketbook long after the patient has been released (or died). The Weavers had suffered financially and emotionally during Charlene's illness . . . .

Charlene's death affected me deeply. It was the first time a patient of mine had died, and she had been more than a number on a chart or a set of lungs on an X-ray. She had been an endearing little girl who had bravely faced an experience that would have terrified most adults. Not only had all my medical knowledge (and the combined knowledge of half a dozen highly qualified doctors) proven useless, but, to the hospital, her death meant no more than the closing of an account.

I knew that, professionally, my attitude was not sound. If I became so involved with all my patients, I would not make a good doctor. Besides, I would probably live the better part of my life in a state of severe depression.

I felt the need to talk to someone and so I turned to Cheryl. She had been in my thoughts constantly since the day she left Chicago. We had written to each other several times, and every one of her letters gave badly needed moral support. That night I called Cheryl in Washington and told her of Charlene's death.

"There was just nothing we could do, Cheryl. It was awful."

"Were you very close to her, Lloyd?"

"Yes. She trusted me. Now I feel as if I've failed her."

"Lloyd, you can't blame yourself. I think I know you well enough to know that you made her last days very happy. You're always making people laugh. And I also know that you're dedicated enough to have done everything you could medically."

"But Cheryl, I feel so useless. I can't help people who are dying, and health care is so expensive that a family like Charlene's will be burdened for years."

"When you're a doctor, Lloyd, you can work to change all that, but now you have to concentrate on the positive side of your profession. Think of all the people who *are* being helped."

Cheryl talked me out of my depression. I loved her and I knew I needed her. I had never felt this way about any girl before and I lacked the sophistication to express my feelings. But I could sense that Cheryl felt deeply about me, too. My life with Cheryl would have to wait until I had finished medical school.

26

The one place I refused to visit was the geriatrics ward. Many of the old people who entered this ward died there, and I wanted no part of it. Fortunately, it was an elective ward and I wasn't scheduled to spend any time on it—until Harry Plum got sick.

Harry Plum had volunteered for the geriatrics section because his grandmother, who was going fast, had requested a preliminary report on the service there. Harry had caught the flu from an arthritic lady named Halley who had died shortly after Harry went home for the weekend. I was assigned to cover for him.

"Why doesn't someone else do it? I've got patients down here," I complained to the resident.

"You've got a girl with a broken leg and a mono case," he reminded me. "It's only for a couple of days."

When I got there, I was told to go directly to Mrs. Halley's room. Her private physician was leaning over her body.

"She's dead," he informed me. "Natural causes."

"How old?" I asked, glancing at the wrinkled face that had borne a smile even into the afterlife.

"Ninety. She had the flu. Who are you anyway?"

"Lloyd Goldman. I'm a student," I explained. "Harry Plum got the flu from Mrs. Halley so he went home for the weekend, and I was told to cover."

The physician left to inform Mrs. Halley's family (which consisted of a housekeeper and a grand-nephew) of her demise, and I returned to the nurses' station to inquire about my duties. They told me that most of the elderly patients demanded quite a bit of attention, usually for trivial complaints. My job was to give a quick exam, checking the pulse, temperature, and throat— things that would make them *believe* they were getting a full examination. Usually they would be asleep by the time I finished. A few of the patients were convinced that medical students, whom they trusted more than nurses, were the *only* ones qualified to change bedpans. I had a running argument with one of the patients, old Mr. Renkold, about who should change his bedpan. I found Mr. Renkold disgusting.

He was seventy-five and dying rapidly of heart disease. Twenty years earlier he had predicted the cause of his death. He was quite proud of his prophecy and made certain that everyone and anyone who entered his private room heard about it.

"You there! Twenty years ago I told my Eileen, my wife, that I would die of heart disease. Ha ha!" His bony finger was resting over his heart, trying to tap. "Now it's coming to pass."

There was absolutely nothing we could do for him. He still smoked like a fiend, and the heart disease was so advanced that it was only a matter of time before a fatal coronary.

"Where is Eileen?" I was trying to make small talk while I took his temperature.

"Dead," he cackled bitterly. "Cancer."

"Did you predict that, too?" I wanted to know if his mystic powers went further than his own illness.

194

"Go to hell!" he sneered. He wheezed quite noticeably when he got too excited. He leaned over the railing on his bed and spit on the floor. This, I learned later, was both a sign of contempt and a necessity to permit him to talk clearly.

It took me no time at all (one day in fact) to learn to hate Mr. Renkold. He would call me every half-hour or so to tell me that the time had come.

"Call Morris Gates," he would tell me. "I want a bronze one." Morris Gates was an exclusive funeral home.

I tried not to get involved with Mr. Renkold in the few days of my geriatric duty. All my other patients were old women who were disappointed because, unlike Harry Plum, I couldn't recite the first thirty words in the dictionary. Mr. Renkold, however, was delighted to learn that I couldn't recite the first thirty words in the dictionary.

"Dr. Plum makes you look like an ass," he confided.

The nurses on this floor told me to ignore the calls from 721 but I was unwilling to take the chance. After all, I had no way of knowing that Mr. Renkold wasn't really in trouble.

"You are a hippie pig," he told me, "and you have no respect for your elders. Look at that hair."

Like a fool, I looked at my hair, which was resting somewhat curiously on my shoulders, as well as kinky hair can rest.

"You must be a Communist," concluded Mr. Renkold. "Do you believe in God?"

"Periodically," I replied, my eyes narrowing, "and if you aren't nice, someone is going to forget to change your bedpan!"

195

Since the nurses on bedpan duty were friendly with me (and detested Mr. Renkold), I was sure I could convince them to "forget" to change his bedpan for a day or two.

The first night I slept on the geriatrics ward, Mr. Renkold decided that medical students weren't supposed to sleep at night. He rang the nurses' station incessantly, complaining each time that he was dying. We knew he was lying.

"Why isn't there an intern on this ward?" I inquired. That was the usual set-up, and I thought it strange that med students should be given such responsibility. Entering the same room with a geriatrics case was considered risky by many veteran physicians.

"No intern in his right mind would stay here longer than a day," explained the nurse. "Besides, the patients all have private physicians."

Mr. Renkold rang the station again and demanded that "that bastard Dr. Goldman get his hippie ass down to 7-2-1."

I went back into the doctors' cubicle and curled up on a couch. Ten minutes later, I was told there was an emergency phone call.

I rushed out and grabbed the receiver. "Hello, this is Dr. Goldman, can I help you?"

"Bastard," hissed Mr. Renkold, who had arranged for an outside line and called the hospital, having me paged from the main desk.

I hung up on him and called the main desk to tell them that I wasn't a resident or an intern and that Mr. Renkold should have the phone removed from his room.

196

A half hour later, a nurse came in and woke me up.

"Seven twenty-one claims this is it."

"So what? He always claims 'this is it.' Tell him to leave me alone or I'll never see him again."

"He's starting to curse . . . loudly, too!"

"OK." I marched down to Mr. Renkold's room.

"Look," I pointed my finger at the withered little man, "you are a hypochondriacal moocher. There are people around here who really need help."

Mr. Renkold just laughed and told me he thought I was quite brave for a man about to be tossed out of medical school. I turned and left him without waiting for another verbal assault. I tried to go back to sleep but couldn't. I felt guilty about being so rough on Mr. Renkold—even if he deserved it.

The next few nights on the geriatrics ward were similar. Mr. Renkold did everything he could think of to make my stay unpleasant. One morning at the close of my first week on geriatrics, I awoke to learn that Mr. Renkold had called the nurses' station for the last time. They found him dead with the buzzer in his hand. I felt no sense of loss, only relief.

As I left the hospital, it occurred to me that my attitude towards Mr. Renkold's demise was the exact opposite of what my feelings about Charlene's death had been. And my new attitude was no less unprofessional. Mr. Renkold may have been a miserable old man, but he was miserable for a very good reason. He was dying and he knew it. He could only sit and wait for the end, knowing that he was a financial burden to his

197

children and a tiresome chore to the hospital staff. Mr. Renkold's bids for attention were his way of rebelling against his dehumanizing situation. In treating my patients, I had to learn to acquire the proper perspective. If not, I ran the risk of becoming either an emotional cripple or an insensitive clod.

27

The first Friday of every month was drug day. A dozen different drug manufacturers would exhibit their wares in the hospital conference room, science-fair style, with each company hawking from its own private booth.

Every pill had a counterpart that created an opposite effect: there were pills to increase the appetite as well as decrease the appetite; there were stimulants and depressants; there were pills to speed up digestion and pills to retard the digestive process; there were even pills to harden or soften the stools of patients with gastrointestinal problems.

The representatives from the birth control companies were the most popular among the medical students because they distributed free samples of everything. There were pills, foams, loops, prophylactics, diaphragms—all different shapes and sizes and colors.

I would have to plan for these monthly drug fairs weeks in advance—family, friends, and patients would phone in their requests. Grandmother Schlessel, reveling in my new-found access to prescription drugs, would demand a brand new laxative every month. Even if she found relief with one brand, she considered herself pressing her luck to stick with it more than a month.

One of my friends at home also requested my help when it came to display time at the hospital. Every month he asked if I could "pick up a couple of packs of rubbers, nothing fancy." Strange as it may sound, the family planning companies that were dispensing rubbers often went to great lengths to make them as colorful and attractive, as well as effective, as possible. It was the old Madison Avenue game of attracting buyers with bright colors and gimmicks. One of the representatives from a local contraceptive company cornered me.

"Sir, you look like a man of vision," he smiled slyly and gave me a wink. "You know the problems of overpopulation, Doctor, and you know that young people today deserve to be told *all the facts* about birth control."

"Right," I agreed amiably. "I need some prophylactics. Any brand will do."

"Any brand will do? No it won't, Doctor. Absolutely not! What school did you graduate from?"

Mystified, I told him that I was finishing up medical school at the university affiliated with the hospital. Rummaging through his products, he came up with a box of rubbers.

"On the tips of these goodies," he declared, "you will find your own school seal! Even the Latin. See there?" He opened the box, but I declined inspection.

"No thanks. Just give me plain ones." I felt like I was ordering a sandwich and I was beginning to wish that my friend would start doing some merchandising on his own.

"What fraternity were you in? We've got all the fraternity symbols and the Greek letters are in relief in the latex . . ."

"No thanks." I grabbed some packages out of the display box and moved on to the next exhibit.

The next guy looked like an unemployed used-car salesman. He was selling anti-anxiety pills.

"Doctor, let me read you the results of a recent study on a group of young elementary school teachers in Allentown, Pennsylvania. Each morning, one half of the sample took a sugar pill before starting class and the other half took our new pill, *Relief*. The study was, of course, double blind . . ."

"Of course," I nodded politely.

"And neither group knew what they were taking. After two years on this regimen, our study proved that 60 percent of those people who took *Relief* were still teaching, while only 43 percent of the sugar-pill group remained with the school system. Therefore, we can safely conclude that *Relief* effectively reduces tension in a busy day of school-teaching." He smiled proudly as he handed me a couple of bottles of *Relief*.

His speech followed none of the logical sequences that were outlined in basic pharmacology, but it wasn't worth analyzing. I collected a couple of notepads and novelty pens while I was there and moved on to another man whose "sale of the day" was antibiotics.

Drug fairs were professional trick-or-treat, legalized pushing. Fortunately, most of the products were relatively safe in the hands of doctors, as long as they remained in the hands of doctors.

One of the most interesting aspects of these exhibits was the placebo displays—various pills given to people suffering from "chronic hypochondria." These pills came in all shapes and sizes so that doctors with problem patients could distribute more than one pill at a time. Most of the time, the pills would miraculously cure the patient, despite the fact that they were absolutely devoid of medication and usually made of sugar or another harmless concoction. In the same vein were salesmen who were trying to unload miracle cough remedies. These fellows were at an obvious disadvantage because they were dealing with doctors, men who supposedly were familiar with their antics.

The old-timers were back-slappers. They chewed gum loudly and confidently and made rigorous attempts to drown out any questions from prospective buyers with more rhetoric expounding the effectiveness of the product. These cough potions were produced in flavors ranging from chocolate (for children), to wine-flavored (for adults), to castor oil (for people who believed that if something didn't taste bad it couldn't be good for you). Despite the fact that they may have sold famously in Western medicine shows of the last century, there is only a minimal market for such syrup today.

The placebo displays were simply one aspect of a much broader phenomenon. People are willing to believe that medical science is capable of curing all maladies—real or imagined.

For example, there is a distasteful tendency for concerned parents and older people to fall into what is popularly called "the magazine syndrome." In essence, the weekly news magazine takes the place of a physician. Every article on heart disease instills new-found optimism in patients with a terminal heart condition. Every new facet of cobalt treatment is studied religiously by cancer victims reading their weekly news magazines. While optimism is always emotionally healthy for the patient, it is not always the most realistic way to face a problem.

Keone, who was still living in the big house with me and five other medical students, lapsed into delirious ecstasy when Linus Pauling revealed his vitamin C-common cold correlaries. Keone was one person who had a common cold an uncommonly large part of the time. Every three or four days he would be freaking out on aspirin and cold tablets, convinced that a preponderance of antihistamines in his system would make him go insane.

"You don't have to go crazy," I reassured him. "Look at this." I handed him the latest copy of a popular magazine that had a feature on Pauling's vitamin C research. Keone devoured the information with glee. That night, he brought four dozen oranges home from the grocery store. Oranges were out of season at the time, but I didn't ask questions.

Keone was certain that drinking a gallon of orange juice a day would absolutely eliminate any chance of his catching a cold on that particular day. What he didn't count on were the side-effects of drinking a gallon or more of orange juice. They were, to say the least, time-consuming. Keone disliked spending two or three hours a day on the toilet so he soon gave up his orange juice fettish and tried the injection technique.

Since he worked in the hospital, he had access to solutions that enabled him to prepare vitamin C. Keone spent hours in the lab until he was certain that his mixture was safe and then returned home late one night beaming and congratulating himself in Hawaiian.

"Are you going to inject yourself with that crap?" we asked him.

"I'm going to wait until I get a cold. Then you'll respect me for all of the trouble I've gone through."

"I don't think that's the way it works, Keone." I was sure that he had misread the magazine article, but I couldn't reason with him.

Keone spent four weeks trying to catch a cold. Finally, after spending a night naked and dripping wet under a tree in the backyard, he awoke with a sniffle.

"I'll show you," Keone threatened as he gave himself the vitamin C dosage. The injections were only slightly more painful than drinking a gallon of orange juice a day.

Three days passed, and Keone still had his cold. On the fourth day, it was gone. "Ah ha!" he exclaimed. "What did I tell you? I'm going to write Dr. Pauling myself and tell him of this great triumph."

I argued with him all morning. "The average length of a cold is about four-to-five days," I explained. "How do you know that you wouldn't have lost it without the vitamin C?"

Keone discounted my argument and proceeded to write to Dr. Pauling. One of Pauling's students wrote back a few weeks later explaining to Keone that, because of studies supporting other conclusions, Pauling's theory was becoming controversial. Keone was heartbroken and resigned himself to living with the common cold for the rest of his life. He also vowed that he would never eat oranges again until the final results of Pauling-type research on vitamin C were published and made it clear that oranges were safe.

28

The room was small. The mahogany table was small. The window was small. The one-way mirror was large, very large, and as I stood before it straightening my tie, I waved feebly to the half-dozen professors seated in an adjoining room watching me and the patient through the glass.

I was on my psychiatry rotation and I was beginning my first interview. I returned to the table and sat down facing the 45-year-old housewife, mother of two, who was going through menopause and had sought counseling at the hospital clinic. The palms of my hands were moist and the sweat on my forehead began gathering conspicuously in my eyebrows. I crossed my legs and smiled at the woman. She smiled politely and I uncrossed my legs and started shifting my weight.

"How do you feel today?"

"Fine, and you?"

"Oh . . . ok, I guess," I said. My legs were shaking so I recrossed them. "Would you like to smoke?"

"No thanks." Her face showed no expression. Her lips were shut firmly, and her eyes looked from me to her lap and back again.

"What brings you here today?" I finally asked her. I glanced up at the mirror. Even if I couldn't see my examiners I wanted to acknowledge their presence so they wouldn't think they were making me nervous.

"I'm depressed, doctor, and I don't know why. Life doesn't mean much to me anymore."

"I know what you mean," I nodded, suddenly noticing that I had been chewing on my thumb while she was talking.

"You do?"

"Well, no, not exactly. But I have been depressed before."

She followed my lead earnestly. "Have you?" she asked, getting the hang of it.

"Yeah, why, just the other day, I got bawled out by one of my professors in class . . ." I halted suddenly. "Uh, listen. You're the one with the problem."

"Of course," she smiled. "As I was saying, ever since last Sunday I have seen no need to get up in the morning. Each day is trivial. I have nothing to do. The kids are all grown up."

I nodded repeatedly. This is a favorite technique and something that is mastered by many psychiatrists at one time or another. Never let the patient know what you are thinking and avoid giving the patient any ideas. I considered myself fairly proficient at nodding and looking serious.

"Life has no meaning?" I asked, using another invaluable maneuver: repeating what the patient says—first, to stimulate more conversation, and secondly, to see if the patient wishes to change his or her story.

"Right," said the housewife, completely composed. "You hit it right on the nose."

I was thrilled by this news, but I couldn't think of any follow-up questions. "Mind if I smoke?" I asked, entirely forgetting the fact that I hated cigarettes. I

206

opened the drawer under the table and chose a filter cigarette. I lit up with poise.

With the cigarette dangling precariously from the corner of my mouth, I continued the interview. "Since last Sunday?"

"Yes. I have refused to attend the bridge club. I have no desire to get my hair done. Half the time I don't even bother to cook dinner before Ted (that's my husband) comes home."

After a minute of profound meditation, I asked, "What does Ted think of all this?" I hadn't puffed on the cigarette once and I noticed that the length of the ash was dangerously long. I searched for an ashtray.

"Ted thinks I'm nuts. That's why I'm here. Ted made me come. He said that a doctor would help me figure out what's wrong."

"Well, we're certainly going to try." I nodded at her confidently and told her to go on. In desperation, I laid the cigarette down on the table to let it smolder and burn out.

"Everyone manages just fine without me," continued the lady. "I feel useless."

Seizing upon this information, I pursued the point. "You feel useless?"

"Yes, that's right."

"Suicidal?" I asked. Before she could answer I panicked, realizing that I didn't want to give the patient any ideas and that this was an idea that would literally end *all* ideas. "I take that back!" I shouted. "Forget I said that."

The woman looked at me suspiciously. "Should I feel that way? Am I supposed to?"

207

"No. no. Of course not," I stammered. "Forget I said that."

"Don't *you* ever feel useless?"

I nodded emphatically. My thumb was back in my mouth and I had resumed perspiring. "Sure. All the time. I mean . . . you know . . . not all the time, but some of the time."

"So you understand?" she begged.

"Of course. Yes ma'am. I know just how you feel." I thought about that statement for a full minute. "Well, not exactly how you feel." Having never been through menopause, I knew that I couldn't have shared all the rigors of that experience. I wanted to be completely honest with my first patient.

About this time, I noticed the mahogany was smoking from my cigarette and I became frantic again. "Can I borrow your coke? Thanks." I dumped her Coca-Cola on the table, putting out both the cigarette and the wood. "Oops." I smiled wanly and started to mop up the mess. "Please go on."

"Do you need some help?" she offered.

"Nah. I'll have this cleaned up in a jiffy." I thought of those six professors, laughing their asses off in the next room. I was on the floor with a handkerchief cleaning up a spilled soft drink when I was supposed to be giving guidance to this disturbed woman who was struggling through the change of life.

"Tommy is eighteen; he's got his own car. Louise just got married to a wonderful man, a banker in New York. Ted works all day (I told you that already), so I have nothing to do. I have no real desire to do anything, either."

I finished up the housekeeping and returned to my place across the table just in time for a nod and a professional, "Hmmm, hmmm."

"That's my problem." She was through now, and it was up to me.

Considering that in all probability I had already failed the "poise" section of my examination, I decided to concentrate on the equally important "patient contact" and "conversational flow" aspects of the interview.

"Have any of your friends gone through this?"

"Yes, but they're no help. They've resigned themselves to old age twenty years before their time. I don't want to resign myself to *anything* . . . I guess that's the problem. I want to be young again."

"What does your husband do for a living?"

"He's an insurance man. It's not the money. We have plenty of money. It's just that he is still so involved in his work. We have the money to go on a cruise or something, but he's too busy. My job as a mother is over, I guess. I don't have the responsibilities I used to have. Maybe if I got out and joined some women's groups—do you think that would help?"

"It might help," I replied. I didn't want to say "yes" or "no" too definitely. Never make any promises to the patient and avoid self-diagnoses. I began to question the logic behind this approach, for it seemed perfectly feasible to me that a patient could cure him or herself.

"There is an emptiness in my life," she sighed and sat back in her chair. "I feel very lonely."

"Every woman has this problem," I informed her,

pretending that what I said was exclusive knowledge, "and every woman has to deal with it in her own way." I paused for a moment, decided that I was making a remarkably sensible statement, and then continued. "Every woman feels depressed at this time in her life."

"Not Margie Henkly."

"Who's Margie Henkly?" I demanded. I felt that my whole remarkably sensible statement had been sabotaged by an unknown, a freak exception to the rule.

"Margie is a girlfriend of mine. Margie had a hysterectomy ten years ago. She's been on hormones since then and she's feeling great."

"Well, *most* women don't have hysterectomies that early in life. Besides, I am sure your friend experienced depression at that time. Your problem is much more common, and the point that I was making still stands: I think you're approaching this whole thing quite maturely." I hoped that "maturely" was the right word to use under the circumstances. "I think this thing will work itself out."

The woman stood up and smiled warmly. "You've been such a help. I feel so much better. Maybe I'll start playing bridge again. There are a million things I can do now that I couldn't do before."

"That's right," I cheered. "You're a new woman!" This display of exuberance on the part of the psychiatric examiner seemed unprofessional, but I didn't care. I was sure that those professors in the next room were disappointed that my first patient hadn't been something more challenging—a schizophrenic, for example.

"You're going to come out of this just fine."

She shook my hand and left. As soon as she was

out of the door, I collapsed into the big leather chair. I was relieved that it was over but still very apprehensive about *my* condition, grade-wise. Dr. Crane, one of the top men in the department, came in. I stood up to greet him, but he motioned for me to remain in the chair.

"Goldman, were you just a little nervous today?" He eyed me closely.

"Well . . . a little," I admitted, "but I thought I recovered just fine."

"Oh, you did," agreed Dr. Crane, "but the Psych Department is going to be pissed off when they see the burn on this table. It's brand new, you know."

"I'm sorry about that. I'll pay for it." I had no intention of paying for it.

"No you won't. You did a good job on Mrs. Kelly. She trusted you, and that's the important thing," Dr. Crane continued. "Most people who come in here just want someone to listen to their problems," he explained. "Everyone thinks he has the exclusive right to depression, suicidal tendencies, senility, and so on. Just a few are genuinely sick. That's the funny thing about this business," said Crane, tapping his finger on the table in front of me. "The really sick people— they are the ones who just can't be convinced that there's anything wrong with them. It's so frustrating." He shook his head and I could plainly see that this aspect of his profession bothered him tremendously. He congratulated me once again and then returned to his five cronies in the next room so they could watch another senior medical student interview another "case."

I wasn't at all convinced that my next interview would be any easier for me, and I was justified in my anxiety. I was on duty in the psychiatry ward of the hospital when I was called down to the emergency room. When I arrived, one of the examination rooms was being guarded by a couple of burly cops. I squeezed between them. There, crouched on the floor under the examination table, were a man and a woman. The woman was in near-hysteria, and the husband was very disturbed about her condition.

"Yes ma'am, can I help you?" I strode nonchalantly into the room with a pad and pencil in my hand. "I'm Dr. Goldman."

"Duck down, Doctor. Quick, duck down!" screamed the woman. She grabbed me by the sleeve and pulled me under the table, too.

"They're after me," she cried.

"She thinks they're after her," said her husband.

"They're after you?" I asked, following that all-important first cue.

"They're after me! The FBI is after me! Look out! They're shooting at us." She put one hand on my head and one hand on her husband's and shoved us both down onto the floor.

"She thinks they're shooting at her," explained her husband.

"How are you today?" I asked, trying to take her mind off the imaginary gun-battle. This question was a standard for all interviews.

"I'm ok," said the husband, thinking I had directed the question to him, "but my wife thinks the FBI is after her."

"Has she done something wrong?"

"Not that I know of. Lena, honey, have you done anything wrong this time?"

The woman shook her head. She glanced furtively at the door and then behind her. Her head was rotating rapidly as she searched for the FBI agents.

"This time?" I asked her husband.

"Yes. This happens pretty often. Sometimes it's the FBI; sometimes it's the Army; sometimes it's the Mafia; sometimes it's the CIA."

"The CIA? Do you come into this hospital often?"

"Down, get down!" screamed the woman.

"Sure," said the husband, "every couple of weeks. One of the residents gives her a shot and she's fine."

I managed, with more than a little difficulty, to do a routine exam on the woman, who refused to come out from under the table. I called one of the residents who explained to me that a certain drug, thorazine, seemed to eliminate all the symptoms of the psychosis. Many psychiatrists today are advocating liberal drug medication for treatment of emotional problems. I accepted the resident's explanation and let him "cure" the woman, who waltzed out of the hospital two hours later saying that her imagination "had obviously gotten out of control."

"FBI! Can you beat that, Leon?" She laughed heartily and took her husband's hand as they left.

During my eight weeks in psychiatry, I did manage to accomplish something in the way of helping a patient. Ironically, my solution to his problem had nothing to do with analysis, medication, or referral. Angel Silvano came into the hospital in what was originally diagnosed as an acute paranoid condition.

They sent him to Psychiatry where we promised room and board for five nights, the maximum allowed.

"Why can't you believe me?" he pleaded. "They've got a contract out on me." Angel had been telling us this ever since he walked into the hospital. "They" were the Mafia. According to Angel, he had started messing around with the wife of the Mafia chieftain in Milwaukee. Her husband had found out and put a price on his head. Angel fled in terror.

"The police won't believe me. The FBI won't believe me. Please believe me! I need help."

At first, I agreed with the intern on the ward who thought the type of "help" Angel needed was more than just protection. We were reasonably sure that he was paranoid.

Angel refused to leave the hospital on the fifth day, so I persuaded the resident on call to let him stay just one more night. I had never seen anyone so scared.

After the sixth night, Angel was literally forced out into the street again. As the policeman was leading him downstairs, Angel stuffed a crumpled piece of paper into my hand. "Here, Dr. Goldman. You'll believe me after you call this number. Ask for Kathy."

It was a long distance number in Wisconsin. I used the hospital phone:

"Is Kathy there?" I asked the female voice.

"This is Kathy. Who's this?"

"Uhm . . . my name is Dr. Goldman at Metropolitan Hospital in Chicago. We just released a man who said that he knew you, a Mr. Angel Silvano . . ."

"Angel?" She sounded elated. "I guess they haven't gotten him yet."

"You mean he was telling the truth about the contract?"

"Oh yes. My husband Frank has a contract out on Angel. I 'spose Angel told you about Frank catching us together in the Chevy. . ."

"Well, no. We thought Angel was making up the whole thing," I answered.

"I've tried to talk Frank out of it. He can be so stubborn."

When I hung up I decided I would warn Angel (if I could find him) that the contract was still valid. That was all I could do.

I ran downstairs to the cashier. Angel had just "checked out" and had left through the double doors in the emergency room. I dashed outside in hot pursuit.

I looked down the street to see my patient, with his jacket pulled up high over most of his head, shuffling down the boulevard clinging to the wall and turning his back on the road every time a car went by. I knew that it would just be a matter of time before the police picked him up and brought him back to Metropolitan for an examination.

"Angel!" I yelled. "It's me, Dr. Goldman. Don't run!"

Luckily, I was much faster than Angel, and I finally cornered him in an alley. I stuffed twelve dollars in his hand and told him to hop a bus and get the hell out of town.

"I called Kathy," I told him, "and you were right. They're still after you."

"Told you so! I told you so! Everyone thought I was a nut!" Angel was jumping up and down and

215

shaking his finger at me. "Now you believe me!"

"Listen," I cried, grabbing him by the arm, "Please get out of town before they find out, ok?"

"Sure. Thanks for the bread! I told you so, didn't I?" he laughed again.

"Bye, Angel." I turned and left him chuckling in the alley. I hadn't gotten very far when I heard footsteps running after me.

"Dr. Goldman, one more thing," shouted Angel from a block away. "You don't think I'm crazy any more, do you?"

"No, Angel," I lied. "Now get out of here!"

"Thanks. Thanks a lot." He turned and trotted in the other direction, obviously relaxed. He took off his jacket and started waving at a bus. "I told you so. Three months. No one believes me. I am not crazy!"

I shook my head and wondered what was going to happen to Angel. Then I shook my head again and wondered what was going to happen to my twelve bucks. "Who's the crazy one?" I chuckled.

29

Surgical rotation, because it was longer than usual and the more prestigious aspect of medicine (for the surgeons), was preceded by a pep talk. The chief of surgery addressed our class in his baritone voice, double-breasted suit, and Cadillac shoes. They were so shiny that I knew he wouldn't put them anywhere but on the floorboard of a Cadillac. What you noticed first about the man were his hands, which were grotesquely large.

"I'll bet he shook up the girls in obstetrics during his rotation there," snickered Keone. "I wonder if they let him do pelvics?"

Fortunately, Dr. Barnes couldn't hear Keone's muttering. If he had, he probably would have put Keone through the floor with one of his grotesque hands.

"People may think we are God-like," began Dr. Barnes, "and that's unfortunate. However, surgery, in my mind, is the *only* specialty that really separates the men from the boys. We do not play with pills or subjective complaints or crackpots or crocks . . . "

A crock is a patient who believes, contrary to all medical evidence, that he or she is seriously ill. These patients are the targets for companies who specialize in placebo medicine.

"Our job is not to placate organic disease," Dr. Barnes rambled on, "but to remove it. We do not monitor a patient whose heart is failing; we give that heart a new blood supply. We do not treat a tumor, experimenting with all kinds of toxic medication; we remove the damn thing. We rip it out!" He was seething by this time and his giant hands were dancing over his head in an emphatic gesture that supposedly made it clear to all of us that surgery was just as melodramatic as television and cinema portrayed.

"Don't get me wrong. *Some*body has to do those other things. But anyone can handle the simple things: delivering a baby, for example. I've seen a student nurse deliver a baby! Surgery—have you ever seen a student nurse do an appendectomy? Remove a gall bladder? How about a tumor in the lungs? You think a student nurse could handle that?"

We all shook our heads confidently.

"Of course not," asserted Dr. Barnes. "You people, beginning today, are going to spend eight weeks in the operating room, under big bright lights, taking orders from temperamental professionals. You'll learn how to use a scalpel—*correctly!* That's right, correctly!" he bellowed. "I know they taught you how to open a corpse in anatomy lab. You may have even mastered the postmortems by now. But, gentlemen, those patients were not living and breathing under your knife!" He wiped his forehead and took a drink of water, convincing me that he had, at one time or another, been an aspiring politician.

"Some of you are not going to specialize in surgery. How many?"

Only a dozen of us were brave enough to raise our hands.

"Good!" he snarled over the microphone. "We don't want you. Most surgeons, most good surgeons, have been trying to get there since they were two or three years old. You've got to want it badly, very badly. You others, the ones who *want* to be surgeons, will be glad to know that from now until the day you die, these internists, these pediatricians, these gynecologists, these . . . general practitioners . . . " Dr. Barnes spit out these words venomously and with obvious scorn for these "lowly" specialties, " . . . these people will depend upon you until the day you die. You—*we*—are the life-savers of medicine!"

I was anxious to get going. I'd been looking forward to surgery ever since Angel Silvano. I needed a change of pace. Besides, Grandmother Schlessel and my parents were all anxiously waiting for me to write home and tell them about O.R. "Don't tell me if it's not like on Dr. Welby," warned my Grandmother.

Dr. Barnes was finishing the lecture. "Twentieth-century surgery is a phenomenon. You are going to be a part of it. You are going to be making it an even greater miracle, *but*, in doing so, you will be defecated on, urinated on, bled on, and vomited on. However, you will learn to save lives. You will learn to save lives!"

A small group of faculty members in the very front of the auditorium applauded loudly. Dr. Barnes nodded "modestly."

"Are there any questions?" None of us dared to raise our hands. "Then, good luck, gentlemen. Each of you is assigned to a surgical team. You're responsible for six patients, whom you must come to know like the

219

back of your hand—their history, physical findings, lab data. You must become an expert in their disease— etiology, anatomy, physiology, diagnostics, signs, symptoms, and treatment. Now you're ready to go."

We applauded politely as he stepped down from the lectern. I was shaken up by the pep talk. Dr. Barnes had seemed so intense in his quest for the "perfect surgical attitude" that I was inspired to race over to the book store to pick up a review book.

There are important differences between medical school now and med school a few years ago. One of them is the review book. The basic differences between the review book and the textbook are size, cost, readability, and simplicity. The only thing that the huge, glossy textbook has in its favor is prestige. When you are in the company of an esteemed professor, it's usually wise to have your dictionary-sized textbook under your arm. However, the thing that really got me through surgery was a three-dollar paperback.

One of the most popular handbooks, a literal life-saver for both patient and student, was the *Washington Manual*, a synopsis of day-to-day medicine. Another very helpful manual outlined briefly and simply the most common surgical emergencies and what to do when they popped up:

APPENDICITIS: History of supraumbilical pain followed by right lower quadrant abdominal tenderness. Scratch the right side of the belly with a pin—the patient is extremely sensitive.

About a dozen or so diseases were outlined briefly

in this manner. If A, on a physical exam, has findings B and C, and if lab results show D and E, then he's got a case of F.

I soon learned that B, D, and E might not always be present and X, Y, and Z might be subbed in. Then it's a whole new ball game. So I missed the diagnoses on the 47-year-old male with appendicitis and, later, the 36-year-old female with gallstones. There is, I concluded after a couple of mistakes, a hell of a difference between the cookbook and the real disease. I would have made these mistakes had I been studying either a twenty-five-dollar dictionary *or* my three-dollar paperback review.

On my way back from the book store, I bumped into a classmate who told me I was being paged by surgery. This meant that it was my turn, my first turn, to see the "temperamental professionals" in action. I dashed up to the surgical suite, got into my gown, scrubbed, and slipped quietly into the O.R.

I was very impressed by what I saw. Three beams of airfield size were lighting the table. Perched on a stool behind the patient's head was the anesthesiologist in a green mask, regulating the vital signs. He controlled the respirator, which mixed into exact proportions the gases being pumped into the lungs: hopefully, enough oxygen to keep the brain alive and, at the same time, enough nitrous oxide to keep the brain asleep. A TV screen monitored the heartbeat; each electronic deflection recorded another contraction.

There were three surgeons crowded around the table. They were dressed completely in blue. The only thing that wasn't covered with *some*thing was their eyes.

221

There were two nurses and an aide standing near the table with the tray of instruments, sponges, and towels.

I tried to drift inconspicuously into the picture, wondering what I was going to do. One of the surgeons spotted me out of the corner of his eye.

"Out!"

I was stunned. "I'm Goldman; they paged me."

"Out! Out! Get out!"

"But I'm Dr. Goldman," I repeated. "They called me downstairs."

"I don't care if you're Christiaan Barnard. Get the hell out of here!" He snarled at me through his mask.

I wasted no time. I exited through the double doors, threw myself into a revolving chair behind the nurse's desk, and smoldered. I knew something was wrong. Just a misunderstanding. I paid my goddam $2500 a year tuition and I wasn't about to be gypped out of my two months in the operating room.

An old nurse saw me fuming. "Get out of there. That's my desk. I know what *you're* mad about."

"You do?"

"Yes, and let me tell you something. You are training in a most sterile profession, young man, and good hygiene is extremely important. Now why don't you be a dear and get a haircut? We can't have your pretty little curls shedding into a wound, now, can we?"

I gritted my teeth and was preparing a rebuttal implicating the nurse in her own argument for sterility when she threw me a plastic headcap. "Wear this."

I had run into trouble more than once about my hair, but it had never seriously jeopardized my progress in medical school. The Chief of Medicine had commented about it once, and a few of my grandmotherish patients would slip me a dollar or two every week for a haircut. When I would return the money at the end of their hospital stay, they would sigh and pat me on the head, "How are you ever going to be a doctor with hair like that?"

So I reentered the suite wearing my sterile shower cap. This time I was accepted with no questions asked.

"That's better, Goldman. How 'bout giving us a hand over here?" said the surgeon who was obviously leading this operation. I was motioned to join four people on one side of the patient. I could see nothing except blue surgical gowns and rubber hands and nurses flitting back and forth between the doctors and the trays of sponges and towels.

"Hold this," said the doctor. "Now pull slightly upward . . . now out, out . . . that's fine, just hold on." I was given a retractor. My job was to pull back and hold about an inch of muscle and fat tissue away from the operative site so that visibility was crystal clear for the surgeons. I could see nothing at all but arms and backs. I squirmed around, carefully holding the retractor, trying to get a look at the patient.

"Nurse," I whispered to the scrub nurse who was handing the chief surgeon a hemostat, "what's this operation?"

"Shhh. Ssshhh," said the scrub nurse and the circulating nurse in unison. The circulating nurse was responsible for seeing that all the necessary tools were sterilized and prepared in time for surgery.

The only part of my body that was doing anything important was my hand, which was holding the retractor. Although I couldn't see my hand, which was between a nurse and one of the assistant surgeons, I assumed that it was somewhere near the action.

"Nurse? Turn on the radio."

I could hardly believe my eyes as the circulating nurse walked to a corner table and turned on a radio. The baseball game was on.

"Goldman? See if you can find out what inning it is. Hand me the scissors."

"You want the scissors?" I asked him.

"Not you. Not you! Nurse, give me the damn scissors and then two clamps, okay? Fine. What's the score, Goldman?"

"No score yet," I reported faithfully, "bottom of the second."

"Let me have a sponge."

"You want a sponge?" I asked. "I can't reach them."

"Not you, Goldman. Damn it, give me a towel, Miss Martin."

"The Mets have a man on third," I told the doctor, whose voice responded favorably from somewhere over the patient.

"Lemme have a ligature and about three clamps down here."

I grabbed a hemostat off the tool table and handed it to the scrub nurse. I was determined to do something important. She threw the clamp back at me and told me they had plenty in the tray at the other end of the table.

"Goldman, your job is to listen to that damn ball game."

"Yes sir," I told the surgeon. "That man on third was picked off by the pitcher."

224

"Damn, not again?" He muttered.

"Yes, sir, he had too big a lead, I guess."

"Goldman, I'm not talking to you. Give me the scissors again and get me a 2-0 silk suture."

Meanwhile, the other doctors were talking among themselves. One of them was bragging about a hole-in-one while the other was describing his new Mercedes and the power-disc brakes that were supposed to stop the car even in a mud-slide. I was beginning to wonder if the operation had been completely forgotten.

In the fifth inning, the head surgeon clapped his hands together. "That's it. Finish this up, will you, Charles? Thanks. What's the score now, Goldman?"

"Six to nothing. Mets are losing."

"Shit," he sighed. "OK, let's do a towel count." This meant that all the instruments, sponges, and towels had to be accounted for before they could finish with the patient. As it turned out, they were one sponge short. Fortunately, it was located under the table where I had accidentally kicked it when the home-run was hit. Suddenly, I realized that my cramped arm was still holding the retractor. The patient was being lifted from the table to a stretcher and I was still clinging to his inch of muscle and fat tissue. "Wait!"

The nurses giggled. They moved away from the table long enough for me to see that they had unfastened my retractor without my knowing it and re-clamped it onto a discarded surgical glove that had been pinned beneath the patient.

"Very funny," I said to the scrub nurse who had masterminded the joke.

"How'd that happen?" asked the surgeon in charge.

"I guess I got a little too involved in the ball game. I'm sorry."

The surgeon laughed. "You've got quite a sense of humor, Goldman. First you pull that stunt—skipping in here with that wig on . . . "

"That was my real hair," I said defensively, "and it won't happen again."

The surgeon laughed. "Real hair! Cute." He turned to follow the nurses and his colleagues out of the O.R. and I called after him.

"Doctor—?"

"Barnes, Goldman. I'm Dr. Barnes."

"Ohhhhh . . . " I faltered. "That was a great lecture you gave today."

"No lecture. Just a friendly talk," he smiled.

"Well, Dr. Barnes, could you tell me what kind of operation was being done here today. I never got close enough to see anything."

"You should have been able to tell from the orders I gave," he said sternly.

"Well, I got here late, and you told me to listen to the ball game so I really didn't hear very much," I explained lamely.

"Guess. Just see if you can guess."

I accepted the challenge. "Hysterectomy? Appendectomy? Vasectomy? Masectomy?"

Dr. Barnes just stood there shaking his head.

"Wrong, wrong, wrong. Goldman, someday you'll learn to keep your eyes and ears open at the same time."

"How am I supposed to learn anything if it's all a big secret?" This was an audacious remark for a man

226

who had just run out of "ectomies" in the guessing game.

"You'll learn. I did. Just for your information, this was an exploratory. No excisions. Too bad you couldn't have been here for a lobotomy or something."

"Too bad," I agreed, following him out of the operating room. After I had disrobed and cleaned up, I peeked back into the O.R. just to get one good look at a naked operating table. I knew that someday I might be working over one and I wanted to get a glimpse of it, sans nurses, anesthesiologists, and doctors. Standing between the double doors, I admired the stainless steel platform for a full minute.

Thus, my introduction to surgery was hardly an exercise in precision. My early assumption, thanks to Dr. Barnes' magnificent speech, was that surgery brought great responsibilities. During my eight-week stay in surgery, my responsibilities consisted of the aforementioned retractor-holding duties, sponge and towel counts, observation during operations, reporting to classes on those operations, and listening to a baseball game. Occasionally, I was "allowed" to cut the thread after the final stitch.

I made one last-ditch effort to get involved in the actual operation itself. Dr. Barnes had taken all the students who had promised to specialize in surgical medicine under his wing and ignored the rest of us. I went to him one afternoon and asked to assist in his next operation. Surprisingly, he agreed.

The next night I found myself in the O.R., standing, as usual, in the background holding a retractor. I was annoyed with Dr. Barnes for having deceived

227

me. Once again I found myself staring at the backs of nurses and surgeons and anesthesiologists while I held my hand, clenched and rigid, over some person's body. I was performing a vital service, true, but I wasn't learning a damn thing.

After about a half-hour, I heard the circulating nurse say something about seeing "the bullet in the stomach wall." This was very encouraging. At least I knew what was going on. Finally, Dr. Barnes called me.

"Give that retractor to Miss Dempsey, Goldman. We don't need it any more." There I stood, with my hands at my sides, waiting for action. "Okay," said Dr. Barnes, "you wanted to help. Get over here."

The sea of nurses and doctors parted as I took my place at the operating table, to the right of Dr. Barnes. The patient was a fairly young male who had been shot in a downtown bar during a fight with his brother. Dr. Barnes briefed me on the patient's condition and what damage the bullet had caused.

"Now, Doctor, we are ready for you!" He pointed to the fleshy patch in the center of the blue sheets that draped the table and the patient.

I noticed, with some bitterness, that the operation was almost over. My job, I was told, was to sew. More accurately, it was to finish sewing. The entry wound (which had been enlarged for the operation so they could look for the bullet) had been stitched up about half way. The sutures were in place; the needles were lying on the linen next to the wound. The wound looked like a half-tied shoe, and my job was to finish tying it.

"This is it?" I asked incredulously.

228

"That's right, Goldman," said my mentor. "Just finish the job that Dr. Kelly started. Three more stitches should do it."

I shook my head, marveling at the magnanimity of Dr. Barnes. He obviously felt that he was doing me a big favor: letting a med student *who wasn't even specializing in surgery* sew up one of his patients. I finished the suturing and tied it.

"May I cut it?" I asked hesitantly.

Dr. Barnes pondered for a minute. "You've done that before, haven't you? Good. Then go ahead."

Carefully, I took the scissors and snipped off the silk excess by the site. It wasn't exactly a test of precision or speed.

"Very good," chortled Dr. Barnes. "Not bad. What did you say you were specializing in, Goldman?"

"I haven't decided yet."

"You've got time yet. Don't worry."

That, unfortunately, turned out to be my most dramatic moment in the operating room as a medical student. The only thing that I really accomplished during those eight weeks was complete and infallible mastery of the retractor. Never once did I let that tool slip so that the bloody, unwanted fat and muscle slapped back into the operative field and obscured the surgeon's view of the site. That was one thing that I could be proud of, I reasoned. Another thing that I could be proud of was that I had stumbled through almost four years of medical school without a catastrophe. The only thing that was now between me and my M.D. degree was the emergency room rotation.

229

30

I was prepared for the worst. I had read all the current best-sellers—the gruesome accounts of the brutality and inhumanity of the emergency room. I was trying very hard to harden myself to the tragedy and murder and drug addiction. I knew I wouldn't be disappointed, and I knew my self-training would be in vain. I knew I'd get sick.

I got sick on my first day. I got sick from the chaos, and I got sick from the patients who got sick. They brought in a three-year-old girl who had been hit by a garbage truck. After the truck had run over her once, it stopped to see what had happened. A pedestrian mistakenly signaled the driver to back up, so he did—right over the little girl again. There was little left of her to pronounce dead, but her family had to be told, and for me, it was Charlene all over again.

The emergency room was divided into two sections—medical to the right, surgical to the left. There were two neatly groomed (and sometimes hostile) clerks who greeted every emergency case. These women had the additional responsibility of deciding, on sight, what kind of treatment a patient needed. Often times they would argue.

Usually, the two clerks would be instructed to

follow simple guidelines. Chest pain patients were sent to the right for medication, stomach pain to the left for surgery, drug addiction to the right for a stomach pump and/or medication, and acute accident victims to the left for emergency surgery. Alcoholics were sent to the right.

Unfortunately, there were no simple symptoms that the simple guidelines could be applied to. Statistically, chest pain means anxiety in younger females but heart disease in older males. Stomach cramps could mean trouble anywhere from the gall bladder to the appendix to the stomach and usually meant scalpel treatment on the surgical side of the E.R.

I was sent to the medical side first. Lined up against the wall, fastened to creaky wooden wheelchairs with handcuffs, was the sleepy "boozer batallion." The people that were awake would talk slowly and amiably with one another while they incessantly hurled verbal abuse at any medical personnel who happened to walk by.

Sam was an unshaven, toothless drunkard with a philosophy degree from Princeton. His primary symptom during his delirium tremens was hallucinations.

"Watch out for the snake! Watch out, Doctor!" He would yell at the top of his lungs.

Sam's shouting bothered me tremendously. Being brand new in emergency, I was apt to take everything for more than it was worth. All the other nurses and doctors ignored his screaming, even though he persisted.

"A spider! A black widow spider!"

Like a fool, I jumped away from the patient I was examining and looked under my shoe.

Rosey was a rich old grandmother who preferred the emergency ward to her penthouse. A widow of twenty years, she had since remarried a solid diet of wine.

"I don't understand why I'm here," she would complain every day when the ambulance delivered her to the E.R. She would call the ambulance service, the same one, about nine every morning and ask for a ride down to Metropolitan. The ride cost her $25, but she believed she was living it up.

We went right down the whole row of drunks, checking them for infections, looking into their eyes, listening to their hearts, and palpating their abdomens. Every now and then one would get obstreperous, but there were always policemen nearby to calm them down quickly.

"Wheezer's Walk" was the asthmatic ward. A wide variety of respiratory patients found their way into this room every day—old people with emphysema, youngsters with food allergies, adolescents with emotional problems. The treatment was relatively simple and it took me only a day or two to learn what to do when one of these puffers came in.

The first thing we did for almost every emergency patient was to get a line into a vein. That way, once treatment was prescribed, we could get the medication directly into the bloodstream in glucose solution. Most of the asthmatics were not in serious shape, so a slow I.V. with a 250 milligram dosage of aminophylline was the standard treatment. The puffers who were having a great deal of trouble breathing were put on a ventilator. There were times when four or five people would be seated in a circle, each blowing into a tube, practicing their positive-pressure breathing exercises, and in between breaths, trading stories about asthma attacks.

Next to the asthmatic room was the O.D. room. Drug addiction in Chicago, as in every other urban center, was a horrendous problem. The regular visits of sick heroine addicts were augmented by a steady stream of drug abusers, most of them on sleeping pills and other tranquilizers, who were semi-comatose or near death.

Making people vomit was a very unpleasant job. After I got the I.V. in and the fluid started for overdose patients, I would have to administer Ipecac instant vomit medicine. If the patients were semi-comatose, the pupils of the eyes were usually constricted and the vital signs were dangerously irregular. For heroin overdoses, as soon as the vital signs were stabilized, I'd have to inject an antidote, naline, that sometimes worked and sometimes didn't, depending on the severity of the original dose of the narcotic. For the drug abusers, the stomach pump was employed if the Ipecac didn't work satisfactorily. This was another one of those unpopular jobs that were saved for med students. Intubating emergency patients for anything usually meant getting puked on (and subsequently sharing the bucket), or spat on, or defiled in some way. Whenever possible, I avoided the O.D. room. When I couldn't avoid it, I would just grit my teeth and try to overlook the depravity of the whole scene, convinced that these patients were not representative of the whole ailing populus. Each overdose case was referred to psychiatry for examination after he recovered, if he recovered, in the E.R.

I had to work in emergency whenever they needed help, and they often needed help late at night and very early in the morning. At the end of my first week on rotation the hospital called me up at about two in the morning and said they needed some help. I wasn't in a very helpful mood, and I was in a less helpful mood when I was greeted by about a dozen people, members of three separate families, upon my arrival. I finally determined that these people were the Miller, the Jenkins, and the Berkowitz families and they all had relatives in different rooms. Benjy Miller was in the O.D. room zonked out on sleeping pills, Mary Lee Jenkins was having severe chest pains, and Leonard Berkowitz was moaning in the corner with a broken arm.

"One at a time!" I shouted, running into the O.D. room to get an I.V. started on Benjy Miller. I was followed by his mother and three sisters.

"We've been waiting an hour," they complained.

Benjy was lying on a stretcher in the corner while two other cases were vomiting in other corners. I ordered the I.V. and told the nurse to get it started.

"I can't get it started," she said.

Losing my composure, I told her she was incompetent.

"You give up awfully easy, nurse. What's your name?" I asked in a sinister tone. "Why can't you get the damn I.V. started?"

I was being impatient with the poor girl because the two families were being impatient with me.

"Because you can't start an I.V. on a dead person," she told me. She was right, too.

I apologized to the nurse and double-checked Benjy Miller who was, as she told me, a dead person by that time. I broke the news to the Miller family as best as I could with eight other people yelling foul things at me. Mrs. Miller accused me of killing Benjy in the overdose ward, and his three sisters started crying and kicking me whenever they could. One of the senior nurses mercifully came along and took the hysterical family out into the waiting room, and I turned my attention to the girl with chest pains, Mary Lee Jenkins.

Mary Lee, only 21 years old, appeared to be having a heart attack. Her parents seemed to think so.

"It runs in the family," they told me.

Mary Lee's boyfriend demanded that he stay with her during the examination. He was even more upset than she was.

"She's all I've got, Doc. Please don't let her die."

Since my confidence had been shattered by Benjy's demise, I had serious doubts about my ability to cure a headache, much less chest pains. I removed Rosey from her wheelchair so Mary Lee could sit down.

"I don't understand why I'm here," complained Rosey as usual, obviously even more confused because the ambulance had brought her in at midnight instead of the customary nine o'clock.

I wheeled Mary Lee towards room #23—heart patients only. Sam, the inebriated intellectual, pointed at my feet.

"Look out for the black widow spider. Look out for the spider!"

I swerved the wheelchair dangerously, attempting to avoid Sam's imaginary spider.

"Be careful, doctor," said Mary's boyfriend. "She's all I've got."

Mary Lee was fiercely holding onto her left breast by the time we reached the cardiac room. She wouldn't let go and I was having a hell of a time getting the stethoscope through her clothes. Her boyfriend was looking over my shoulder intently. When I ordered Mary to take off her jacket and blouse, she said that it hurt too much when she tried to move.

Suddenly, room #23 was invaded by the paramedical heart team. The paramedics brought oxygen masks, an electric cardioverter, an X-ray machine, and an electrocardiogram unit. After all this was attached to my patient, I noticed that the Berkowitzes had violated hospital regulations and had entered the cardiac room. They were ranting and raving that brother Leonard was going to need an amputation if I didn't hurry. I had them expelled and proceeded to try to undress Mary Lee Jenkins, who was still holding on to her damn breast.

The resident of the emergency ward finally came to the rescue, striding in with a cup of coffee and a cigarette.

"Get the wires and the mask off this girl," he ordered. The paramedics complied, scowling at me the whole time.

"She's all I've got . . . don't let her die . . . don't give up now!" pleaded her boyfriend.

"I'm not going to let her die. She's going to be fine."

The resident brushed me aside and spoke to the girl softly for about five minutes about relaxing, not taking life so seriously, and trying to ignore her parents once in a while. She got up off the examination table with a smile on her face, releasing her breast.

237

"Bless you," praised Mrs. Jenkins as I walked out of the room.

"I didn't do anything," I explained, "bless him." I thumbed toward the resident, who was busy apologizing to the cardiac team for my blunder in bringing a patient suffering from anxiety to the emergency area for heart patients.

"I'm sorry," I told the resident later, "but this place was a mess and I thought she was really in trouble."

"You're a student, right?"

"Yeah. I get my M.D. in a month or so."

He smiled at me. "When you get a female with heart pains, especially a very young female clutching one of her breasts, try to calm her down. In many cases, she may be just high-strung. It's a very common symptom of anxiety and there's no need to get upset. Okay?"

I nodded sheepishly and went back to the Berkowitzes. Tonight's a bad night, I thought to myself. One death and one misdiagnosis to my credit. Determined to do it right, I proceeded to set Leonard's broken arm with all the care and precision one might ask for in major heart surgery. When I had finished, I accepted with no little modesty the praise from his family.

"Just like on TV," beamed his mother.

"What's your name, Doctor?" asked Leonard's over-protective sister. "You did a fine job on Lenny."

"My name is Goldman, and I'm not quite a doctor."

Stunned, the family backed away from me, shielding Leonard and his slinged arm. They started inching towards the exit.

"Not a doctor?" whimpered Leonard's mother.

"It's all right," I pleaded. "In one month I'll be a doctor. For real."

"A quack! Mother, did you hear that? Daddy knows a good lawyer doesn't he? Good." Lenny's sister ranted on about lawsuits and malpractice charges. Her parting remark was, "If his arm heals crooked, you're in big trouble *Mister* Goldman."

I went home for the rest of the night, disconcerted by the knowledge that I had pleased no one, least of all Benjy Miller's family who thought I had killed him in the overdose room. It was also very difficult trying to fall asleep knowing that it was quite possible that Leonard Berkowitz's arm might be healing crooked at that very moment.

The next night was no better—no better because they called me about the same time and reminded me that I had "volunteered" to help any time they called. When I arrived at the E.R., the place was crawling with alcoholics. At the same time, because of a terrible accident on the expressway, several victims who needed surgical help were admitted into the medical section since there was no more room in the surgical section.

Because the resident and the interns were so busy with the accident victims and alcoholics (Saturday night was a biggie for drunks), they asked me to check any D.O.A.'s (Dead on Arrivals) that came in. That is, when a patient was brought in near death, or virtually dead, I was supposed to do the final exam, pronounce him dead, and find a resident to sign the blue sheets. This always seemed unfair to me. If I did all the work (which took about five seconds), I should get credit for pronouncing the man dead. Legally, however, I would have to wait a month before I could sign the final papers.

This is how I got involved in the mortician's battle. Some of the less prosperous funeral homes send out "feelers" to the emergency room. When someone dies, they are the first ones to approach the stretcher expressing their condolences to the grieving relatives. The key to their attack, one apprentice mortician confided to me, was getting to the mourners within five minutes after the victim passed away. Under those circumstances, he explained, no one would say no to anything except an autopsy.

A private ambulance brought in a D.O.A. candidate early in the morning. It was another elderly man who had suffered a devastating coronary in his sleep. He was still quivering when they showed him to me, but by the time they got him to the cardiac room, I knew he was dead. While the paramedical team worked on him, a young man dressed in a business suit questioned me carefully in the waiting room. He asked what were the "chances of the old guy pulling through."

I assumed he was a member of the immediate family, so I consoled him. "He's got about a 50-50 chance." The young man's face fell and he continued pacing back and forth, chain-smoking furiously. I returned to cardiac room #23 to check on the old man; they were wheeling him out, blue as an icicle, when I arrived. I accompanied the body into the hall. The young man rushed up to me.

"Is that him? Did he . . . die?"

I nodded solemnly. "I'm sorry. We did everything we could for him. He fought hard . . . "

My speech was interrupted by my listener, who latched onto the stretcher and started dragging it out of the exit.

"Where are you going?"

He stopped for a second and handed me a business card: Powdery Pines Funeral Gardens.

"No you don't!" I grabbed the other end of the stretcher. "I thought you were family."

The young man released the stretcher and addressed me indignantly. "You are obviously new here. The same ambulance that brings a patient in *must*, under all circumstances, deliver him from the hospital to the funeral home."

"Bullshit. When the family arrives, you can ask them."

A middle-aged man approached me from my blind side. "Sir, did you say family? I'm family."

Relieved, I explained to the little man about the death of his "relative." He seemed composed and agreed to take care of the funeral arrangements himself. I got him to sign for the body and headed back to the medical section.

The young man grabbed me before I got through the double-doors and pointed towards the emergency entrance where I saw the little middle-aged man leading the coronary victim into a hearse. I ran outside and once again retrieved the body.

"You lied to me, you fraud."

"Business is slow," he explained, throwing up his hands.

The middle-aged man and the young man sat down

together on a bench in the waiting room, presumably hoping for another D.O.A. over which they could wrestle. The family of the deceased finally arrived and signed all the necessary papers. This time, I was careful to make sure that they were indeed relatives. Maybe I was too careful—a grieving daughter is understandably upset when she has to show three I.D.s just to claim the body of her father. It was no wonder she denied the hospital the autopsy.

The emergency room of the hospital is a micro-cosm of the more sordid aspects of a city. There were guts and blood and bullet wounds and knife wounds and rape victims and victims of sadism and group sex criminals and junkies and V.D. and mangled acute victims. Can anyone get used to this? Can anyone learn to make absurd judgments and reorder their priorities so that the drug addict waits in line behind the knife victim who waits in line behind the gunshot victim who waits in line behind a man with an acute bleeding ulcer who'll die in shock without a transfusion?

There was meek Mr. Denmark who came in with chest pains and there was outspoken Mrs. Houghton who had a painfully fractured leg. Mr. Denmark insisted the screaming woman should be treated first. Thirty minutes later when I had finished setting Mrs. Houghton's leg, Mr. Denmark was lying dead on the floor. He had suffered a heart attack. Mrs. Houghton limped happily out of the E.R. with no complaints. Mr. Denmark didn't complain either. I felt awful when I saw him there on the tile, his face in a pud-dle of saliva and perspiration and his body cold as stone. I had let myself be swayed by Mr. Denmark. Mrs.

242

Houghton was in excruciating pain—her leg had been snapped like a match. She was suffering much more visibly than Mr. Denmark, yet, paradoxically, he died and she lived. This was something I had to accept, and I wasn't sure I could.

Surgery in the E.R. was much looser than it was under Dr. Barnes. The E.R. staff needed all the help they could get. After two weeks in medicine, they switched me to the other side of the ward for a little stitching. Dr. Barnes would have been proud of me. I became quite proficient at quick, concise, and relatively painless suturing.

In between minor surgical operations, I was allowed (only in the presence of nurse supervisors) to do pelvic exams on girls complaining of venereal symptoms. This was not one of my more enjoyable chores. Despite the rubber gloves and sterile instruments and disinfectants, every time I had a patient with positive symptoms, I would wince when inserting my hand. Just one flaw in the surgical glove would mean a contaminated hand. It would be a nightmare trying to explain gonorrhea of the hand to Mrs. Seltzer or grandmother. In reality, my chances of getting the disease in this manner were practically non-existent, but for the first half-dozen pelvics I was very, very cautious, often carrying preparatory hygiene to absurd extremes. One of my fellow students suggested I spray Lysol in the vagina before the exam; I had the good sense to recognize his sarcasm before I got into trouble.

The emergency room is bittersweet. Somehow, the people who work there day in and day out manage to develop a necessary insensitivity to tragedy while retaining a much needed sense of humor. There were a few light moments for me. Once, I had to explain to the genitourinary specialist at four in the morning how a young man managed to get shot in the penis by a jealous girlfriend. There was a three-year-old child who came in with a rare condition: lima beans in the ears. He had shoved a lima bean in each ear and it disappeared down the external opening. Both of these operations were somewhat delicate, and fortunately, I was not required to do anything more than watch.

My E.R. duty lasted a month. By the time it was over I had learned to remain calm in crises, to make critical judgments quickly and efficiently, and to accept death as an ugly but inevitable aspect of emergency medicine. When I walked out of the emergency room after four weeks, I had gained some invaluable experience and a little confidence. Before that time, I had needed constant reassurance from Cheryl to dispel my sense of inadequacy. With every new experience, I had called or written her for moral support. She had always responded, seeing me through every crisis. Now I sat down to write a different kind of letter. I invited her to the graduation ceremony, less than a week away, and added that now, at last, we could spend more time together. Was it really almost two years since her last visit? At the time, we had promised each other not to wait this long.

Well, I thought as I dropped the letter into the mailbox, we'll just have to make up for lost time.

31

"So, you're a nice Jewish doctor," said Grandmother Schlessel, "finally. Eight years is a long time, Dr. Goldman."

"Yes," I replied, "eight years is a very long time." Why hadn't Cheryl come? She hadn't even answered my letter.

"We'll eat lunch at Bamberg's again," laughed my grandmother, "and this time I won't be fibbing when I introduce you as *Doctor* Goldman, my grandson."

My father shook my hand. "I want you to know that your mother and I were behind you the whole way, Lloyd. This was a big decision you made, going into medicine."

At this point my memory failed me. Had I made that decision? I must have had some help.

"Lloyd, you've done just wonderfully." My mother gave me a hug and shed a few tears on my shoulder. "What's it going to be now, Dr. Goldman?"

"What do you mean?"

My mother looked at my father in consternation. "Well . . . remember our phone conversation of a few years ago? The time has come to decide—between Chevy Chase and Appalachia."

I turned my back on my family for a second. "I'll let you know in a year," I said brusquely, "after internship. In the next year I'll be working three hospitals and I'll see a big selection of patients. I'll make up my mind then."

I was, in Grandmother Schlessel's words, a "nice Jewish doctor, finally." I didn't feel very nice; I didn't feel particularly Jewish; and least of all did I feel like a doctor. The only part of Grandmother's exclamation that rang true was the word "finally." God, did I feel "finally." It had been a long time. Eight years it took me to live up to her lie in Bamberg's Delicatessen. Eight years of fetal pigs, grade-grubbing, twenty-four-hour urine specimens, Charlene, and Angel Silvano—and there was my family—waiting to hear if I was going to end up in Chevy Chase or Appalachia.

Harry Plum, naturally, had graduated first in the class. He still couldn't tie his own shoelaces. Keone had finished third or fourth and vowed not to let me forget it, despite the fact that I already had. It was either third or fourth, though. Lloyd Goldman had graduated around twenty-ninth, although my family's estimates ranged from first to fourth.

After the graduation ceremony, which was somewhat of an anti-climax, my family hopped on a jet and headed back to Washington. I returned to my newly rented apartment as a full-fledged intern to brood over Cheryl. She hadn't attended my graduation. She hadn't even answered my letter. I knew something was wrong even though I had been pretending all along that there was a simple explanation for her failure to respond to my invitation. I wanted to find out the truth, but at the same time I was afraid. I must have picked up the phone twenty times that evening. I'd dial all but the last number and then hang up. I knew it was up to Cheryl to call *me*.

It was very late when she called. Her subdued tone confirmed my worst fears.

"Lloyd?"

"Hello, Cheryl."

"I guess I should have called sooner, Lloyd. But I've been afraid to."

She waited a second to see if I would respond, but when I didn't she continued.

"The past couple of days—since I got your letter—have been just miserable for me. I really wanted to be at your graduation, Lloyd. That's all I've thought about for months. But I finally decided it would be better if I wasn't there."

"Why?" I asked as a cold wave of fear swept through me.

"Because there's someone else, Lloyd."

Even though I had been expecting those very words, I felt stunned. This just can't be happening, I thought. Not now, after all this time.

"I didn't want it to happen, Lloyd," Cheryl continued, desperately. "I didn't even know it *was* happening. I worked with Jeff. I saw him every day. I love him. I can't help it."

I felt numb. I didn't answer.

"We're going to live together. Mother is taking it hard, but eventually she'll accept us. Please believe me, Lloyd. I cared about you and I still care about you. We were so close. I hope that won't change. I hope we'll always be friends."

The numbness was wearing off and the pain was

247

beginning. I didn't know what to say so I simply repeated what she had just said. "I hope we'll always be friends, too. Good-bye, Cheryl." Then I hung up— without waiting to hear her good-bye . . . .

My first impulse, of course, was to blame Cheryl. I had been stuck in Chicago, busting my ass in medical school, and she had been home in Washington, running around with another guy. At least, that's how I rationalized her leaving me. I was deeply hurt and wallowed in self-pity for quite some time. A couple of weeks after her phone call, I sat down to write her, intending to point out how unfair she had been. Writing that letter caused me to reflect upon the last four years. What had happened? I had become deeply involved in medicine—so deeply involved I had time for nothing else. I should have spent more time with Cheryl, but instead I spent all my time studying. Cheryl, in the meantime, had fallen in love with someone else. I was to blame. But in spite of everything, I knew that if I was offered the opportunity to relive the last four years, I wouldn't live them any differently. I tore up the letter. Somehow, after all those years, I had to forget Cheryl Seltzer.

32

On Monday morning, internship started, and I *had* to push all personal problems aside. Well, I mused philosophically, maybe I'll never find a pair of panties wrapped around my shaving cream again, but by the same token, I'm free of Mrs. Seltzer.

Being an intern meant returning to the emergency room. I felt very much like a medical student, only now I had a little more authority. Now that I had my M.D., I actually got to sign my name on the blue sheets when I pronounced people dead. When Mr. J.S. Jones died, he was my first legitimate death, and I wanted to make sure that I got everything right. My first D.O.A. had to be just perfect.

"He's still warm. I can't pronounce this man dead," I concluded.

"Mr. Jones IS dead. We just had the heater on in the hearse," the irate ambulance driver told me. Many funeral homes provide ambulance service in an attempt to get business.

"Room #23 and fast!" I shouted at the orderly. The emergency cardiac arrest team came charging in. First: inhalation therapy—pushing oxygen and pumping the heart. The nurses were preparing the intravenous meds. The resident rushed in and started shocking the heart with the electric cardioverter. The lab technicians drew blood for emergency analysis. The E.K.G. was turned on, and it registered a "flat line." Mr. J.S. Jones was dead.

I returned to the waiting undertaker's assistant who had brought Mr. Jones in. "I'll give him one last check, and then you can have him."

"What do you want, doc? The old guy's dead!"

"We have to make sure."

The attendant leered at me. "You're new here. An intern, right?"

We argued and exchanged obscenities before I returned to room #23 and found the team working feverishly on Mr. J.S. Jones again. It turned out that after they had taken all the wires off, Mr. Jones had opened his little dead eyes and sighed plaintively.

"I was right. He's alive!" I screamed triumphantly and started pounding on his heart. The technicians attached all the machines again and the electrocardiogram went flat for the second time. Since each of these obviously futile resuscitation efforts cost the hospital close to $500, I knew that I wouldn't be able to talk them into resuscitating Mr. Jones a third time, even if he got up and demanded it himself. I wheeled the stretcher out into the hall for my final once-over.

"That's twice, Doc. I told you he was dead," scoffed the attendant.

I bent over Mr. J.S. Jones' body and checked his pupils, which were dilated and fixed, indicating that he was, indeed, dead. I was still determined to make perfectly sure. I checked for a pulse and found none. I checked for respiration; Mr. Jones was not breathing. I shined a light in his eyes for the second time; there was no pupil reflex. I stood up and faced the attendant.

"This patient is dead."

"No kidding."

"Where is the family?"

"No family," he shot back at me.

"Liar!" I shot back at him.

"Quack!" he shot back at me.

I saw my friend from Powdery Pines sneaking furtively through the double doors, and I waved to him. "I got one for you!" While the original attendant cursed and fumed, the hearse from Powdery Pines carried off Mr. J.S. Jones. I proudly affixed my signature, followed by a clear, bold "M.D.," on the bottom of the blue sheet. What I didn't tell the first guy was that Mr. Jones' family had called long-distance from New York and, refusing an autopsy, had asked specifically that the body be sent to Powdery Pines.

Since I was working three different hospitals, I was forced to familiarize myself with three different emergency codes. One of the hospitals was nonchalant about summoning a doctor for a non-emergency. The normal paging system was very polite: "Dr. Goldman, please." Just once. When an emergency arose, they would announce, "Dr. Goldman, Dr. Goldman," dropping the "please."

One of the other hospitals would say, "Dr. Goldman, STAT" when an emergency arose.

The third hospital revised its code so that "Code Blue!" was the signal for action for both the doctor being paged and for any available medical personnel. They had a special code for cardiac arrests. It was "Doctor, C.A.," and any doctor was supposed to answer the call.

I ran into a little trouble when I answered the

"Code Blue" in one hospital, and it turned out to be a delivery instead of an emergency. In another hospital, if they didn't say "please" I would rush to the nurse's station only to find that they never said "please" at that particular institution.

I was very fortunate in not having to work the three hospitals at the same time. When I wasn't working the E.R. at Metropolitan, I was treating patients at a private hospital. There was a major difference between the fourth year med student and the intern: The responsibility for these patients was mine, entirely mine. I determined the diagnosis, the treatment, and the amount of attention given to a patient. At first, it was very nerve-wracking; I didn't feel like a doctor. I still felt like a medical student. After eight years, it was going to be difficult to break out of the harness. I wasn't fighting for A's and B's anymore (as Dr. Benson had warned me), I was fighting for that proverbial "life and death" decision. If someone got worse, or died, then there was only one person to blame, and that was me.

My most dramatic bout with this kind of uncertainty came early in my second month of internship, when a patient with a mild case of pneumonia entered the hospital. I examined him thoroughly and observed that he had a low hematocrit (anemia) and a slight fever. I wanted to draw blood cultures to check for septicemia (blood infection), just in case. I was, however, fairly certain that this was an uncomplicated case of pneumonia. Just to make sure, I asked another intern to come in and take a look at the patient, a white forty-year-old male.

"He's got a heart murmur," said the intern,

listening to the man's chest.

I listened for it. "I don't hear a thing."

"It's Grade One."

I bent over and listened into the stethoscope once more, but I still didn't hear the murmur. The intern must have had those super-sensitive ears so common in a young house officer.

I was off duty that night when the patient's condition worsened rapidly and he died. I was astonished the next morning when the same intern told me.

"How could he die? It was uncomplicated pneumonia, that's all."

The intern shook his head gravely. "Are you sure? Heart murmur, low hematocrit, fever—bacterial endocarditis . . . septic shock!"

"I didn't hear a murmur," I argued, "and his hematocrit was only thirty-six." The intern had implied that I had missed the diagnosis of the endocarditis, which is an infection of the heart valve.

"We'll see, won't we?" He was talking about the autopsy. Thursday was pathology conference day. Important medical personnel from all over the hospital sat in on an autopsy to hear the intern review the case history of the deceased (what he treated him for and why, etc.). This was almost as bad as med school interviews. The Chief of Medicine was on hand to question me.

I arrived in the postmortem minutes after they had finished removing all the bodily organs from the bladder to the brain. They were lying on a huge white tray covered by a towel. My patient's body, empty as a shell, had already been removed from the table.

I squeezed myself into a corner. After reconsidering the case, I was petrified. Maybe there *was* a heart murmur. Maybe there *was* bacterial infection on the heart valve. Maybe his blood *was* seeded with infection. Maybe I had let my patient die in septic shock by postponing rigorous antibiotic treatment. I blamed myself mercilessly as I sat there and watched the radiologist and pathologist and the Chief of Medicine examining the organs. I had made a horrendous mistake by missing the diagnosis, *if* I had missed the diagnosis.

"Dr. Goldman," said the Chief of Medicine, "give us your synopsis of the case."

I cleared my throat and stood up. "Well, this was a 40-year-old white male who came in with lobar pneumonia. His chest X-ray revealed an infiltrate in the right lower lobe, so I treated him for pneumonia. This patient was also slightly anemic."

"Was there a heart murmur?"

"Dr. Kertz thought he heard a Grade One diastolic murmur at the left sternal border. I didn't hear it, though."

The radiologist stood up with an X-ray of the lungs and pointed out the right lower lobe infiltrate. The pathologist then took the towel off the tray of organs. All eyes were on the heart. If they found damaged valves, then I had misdiagnosed: I had killed the patient by not starting treatment for the endocarditis.

"We found nothing on the valves," explained one of the other doctors, who had risen from a seat by the table. "This is a perfectly normal, healthy heart." I gasped out loud.

A lab technician approached the Chief of Medicine

and handed him the results of the cultures, which he read aloud: "All six blood cultures are negative."

I felt as if a tremendous weight had been lifted from me.

The conference wasn't over, however. Something had obviously gone tragically wrong with my pneumonia case during the night, and the autopsy would undoubtedly reveal the cause of death. The truth was lying on the white metal tray. I was asked to "have a look at the brain."

"There's a blood clot here," I observed. "An aneurysm."

"Are you asking us or telling us?"

I hesitated. "I'm suggesting the strong possibility of an intracranial bleed from the rupture of a berry aneurysm." This meant that one of the blood vessels to the brain ballooned out and burst, killing the patient.

All the white coats in the room looked at each other. I felt clammy and nervous, the same kind of nervousness that I had experienced years ago during a lab quiz or an identification test in anatomy lab.

Finally, the Chief of Medicine announced to the room: "This man did not die in septic shock. This was a freak case. You want to summarize, Goldman?"

"This was a 40-year-old white male who was admitted with right lobar pneumonia and died of a totally unrelated, and unfortunately unpredictable, problem—an intracranial bleed secondary to a ruptured berry aneurysm."

My observers nodded their heads in concurrence; the ordeal was over. My M.D. degree had brought with it increased responsibility, increased personal satisfaction, and respect—respect from many people who wouldn't have listened to a third or fourth year medical student . . . .

I'm still adjusting to the change in people's regard for me. Now that I sign M.D. to my name, I'm supposed to have all the answers. People no longer distrust my decisions in the emergency room and I never have any trouble authorizing a D.O.A. And when I'm introduced as Dr. Goldman, everyone at the party rushes up to me with a minor affliction I'm expected to cure with some casual advice or a hastily scribbled prescription. People refuse to believe that I can make a mistake, that I can accidentally harm them.

I'm also having difficulty acquiring the "proper" professional attitude. I still get nervous—just as nervous as I was when I waited for my grade report after that first year of college. I still get scared—just as scared as I was when my bladder almost exploded at Dr. Evans' dinner party. I still get sick—the same kind of sickness that gripped me the first time Ethel's eyes opened in anatomy lab. As a doctor, however, I can't appear nervous or frightened and I have to suppress the sickness in my gut. When I know someone is going to die, I have to hide that knowledge; I can't let the family see it in my eyes. Am I cold and mechanical and indifferent? I behave coldly, I operate mechanically, and I accept sickness and death indifferently because I must. In twenty years I may very well be hardened to it all, but I doubt it. I've never met a doctor who was. Right now, I'm clinging tenaciously both to my ambition to be a good doctor and my desire to remain a sensitive human being.

256

My determination is being undermined at every turn by social constraints beyond my control, forces which first began to affect me as an undergraduate. Nine years ago, I sought a medical education with a naive idealism characterized by all the traditional humanitarian goals. While training under some of the most renowned physicians in the country, I became knowledgeable in the complex physiological and biochemical processes which make the human body tick. I learned a new language and experienced invaluable hours of clinical practice. At the same time, however, my idealism was slowly eroded by influences in my environment.

First of all, there was the self-defeating competition. As an undergraduate, I believed, along with everyone else, that the key to survival was my fraternity's exam file; when applying to medical school, I was tempted by the guarantees of counseling agencies; and before being interviewed by admission panels, I prepared stacks of "appropriate answers" to preconceived questions.

Secondly, financial demands clouded my priorities. Whenever I protested spiraling tuition fees, I was reminded that one day I would be a well-to-do and "successful" doctor. Every time I applied for another loan, I became more securely trapped by the system. Now, although I don't want to be motivated by financial considerations, I find myself thousands of dollars in debt. I'm not justifying the high cost of medical care; I'm condemning the financial structure which perpetuates those prohibitive costs.

Finally, I was forced to confront the limitations of

257

medical science. Advances are always being made, but they will never compensate for the failures—the little girl who died in hypoglycemic shock because the cause of her disease could not be determined. I also cannot escape a sense of personal failure. It weighs heavily each time I sit in the autopsy conference waiting for the pathologist to reveal his findings on a patient of mine who was alive six hours earlier. The knowledge of those limitations is what makes me uncomfortable when someone salutes my title.

The competition, the financial paradoxes, and the incessant wavering between medical success and medical failure continue to mold my character. Unfortunately, they are as much a part of my career as the sense of responsibility and the personal satisfaction. However, I'm fighting them all the way, trying to maintain the idealism of that nice Jewish boy who became a nice Jewish doctor—finally.